PENGUIN CANADA

ON FIRE IN THE KITCHEN

Ted Reader, author of the bestselling *Hot, Sticky and On Fire* and *Sticky Fingers and Tenderloins,* is host of *King of the Q* and co-host of the U.S.-based barbecue show *The Grilling Meister.* Ted, known for making barbecuing easy and entertaining, has earned a reputation not only for his inventive grilling recipes, but also for his planking technique. For years Ted hosted the grilling/food section of the TV show *Cottage Country,* which aired on CBC and CTV, and on PBS in the United States.

Throughout his career, Ted has worked as team chef for drivers Adrian Fernandez and Roberto Moreno of the CART Racing Series, and as an executive chef for some of Toronto's finest restaurants. He was chef at the Skydome Hotel, and the executive chef of President's Choice®, where he helped develop such products as the PC Tournament Ribs and PC Thick and Cheesy Burgers, along with the recipes in the *Dave Nichol Cookbook* and the *PC Barbecue Cookbook.* He is also the author of *The Complete Idiot's Guide® to Grilling with Ted Reader, Cottage Cooking Cookbook, Sticks and Stones,* and *Cottage Country Television's Grilling.* Ted's U.S. cookbook, published by Alpha and based on *Sticky Fingers and Tenderloins* and *Hot, Sticky and On Fire,* launched in spring 2003. Most recently, Ted has appeared on *Regis and Kelly.*

Also by Ted Reader

Hot and Sticky BBQ (U.S. edition)

Hot, Sticky and On Fire

Sticky Fingers and Tenderloins

The Complete Idiot's Guide® to Grilling with Ted Reader

Sticks and Stones

The Cottage Cooking Cookbook

TED READER
ON FIRE
IN THE KITCHEN

the King of the Q
takes it indoors

PENGUIN
CANADA

PENGUIN CANADA

Penguin Group (Canada), a division of Pearson Penguin Canada Inc.,
10 Alcorn Avenue, Toronto, Ontario M4V 3B2

Penguin Group (U.K.), 80 Strand, London WC2R 0RL, England
Penguin Group (U.S.), 375 Hudson Street, New York, New York 10014, U.S.A.
Penguin Group (Australia) Inc., 250 Camberwell Road, Camberwell, Victoria 3124, Australia
Penguin Group (Ireland), 25 St. Stephen's Green, Dublin 2, Ireland
Penguin Books India (P) Ltd, 11, Community Centre, Panchsheel Park, New Delhi – 110 017, India
Penguin Group (NZ), cnr Airborne and Rosedale Roads, Albany, Auckland 1310, New Zealand
Penguin Books (South Africa) (Pty) Ltd, 24 Sturdee Avenue, Rosebank 2196, South Africa

Penguin Group, Registered Offices: 80 Strand, London WC2R 0RL, England

First published 2004

(WEB) 10 9 8 7 6 5 4 3 2 1

Copyright © Ted Reader, 2004
Interior Colour Photographs © Per Kristiansen, 2004

Manufactured in Canada.

NATIONAL LIBRARY OF CANADA CATALOGUING IN PUBLICATION

Reader, Ted
    On fire in the kitchen : the king of the Q takes it indoors / Ted Reader.

Includes index.
ISBN 0-14-301601-6

1. Cookery. I. Title.

TX840.B3R4225 2004   641.5   C2004-902222-9

Visit the Penguin Group (Canada) website at **www.penguin.ca**

To my love, Pamela,

and to all of my family and friends: you are my inspiration.

Thanks for all the flavours.

Contents

Acknowledgments

To my family and friends, who endured hours of tastings, consumption and patience: cheers and thanks.

And much thanks to:

Pamela: You are the reason for all that I do. Your love and patience with the messy kitchen days, the weird smelly fish days and all the excess food in general is just one of the ways that you are ever supportive. P.S. It was Mike!

Chef Mike McColl: Thanks for all the great help and delicious recipes. You spent endless time and effort testing and writing, plus many other tasks. Your contribution to this book and all the wonderful days is most appreciated. You rock!

Sigal: What can I say? Without your persistence and dedication this book would never have been written. You put up with my illegible, tiny "chicken scratched" notes on various snippets of paper, my arrows that sometimes led nowhere and my general craziness.

King of the Q TV: Kirk, Leslie, Joe and Robin—What can I say? Our show is now our show. Yahoo!

Ron McAvan of Celtrade Canada: To your culinary creations that make *King of the Q* all about grilling, glazing, dipping and licking.

Steve Mintz at Uni Foods, Plumrose and Rupari: My best supporter. Thanks.

All the folks at Napoleon BBQ: We grill excitement!

Reynolds Foil: Your Release Non-Stick Aluminum Foil is the newest and best kitchen essential.

Heritage Salmon: Thanks, Andrea and Adam.

Jack Daniel's: Mmmmm, J. Delicious.

Nicole de Montbrun and the folks at Penguin: Thanks again for your continued support and patience.

Per Kristensen Photography: As usual, Per, your photos are good enough to eat.

Foreword

"The creation of a new recipe does more for human happiness than the discovery of any star!"
—Jean Brillat-Savarin

When Ted asked me if I would write the foreword to his latest book, I was delighted. Ted and his wife, the lovely Pamela, are among my dearest friends. And one look at this book and I knew it would be easy. Instead of *On Fire in the Kitchen*, it should be called *Saturday Night at Ted and Pam's*. As awe-inspiring as some of these recipes are, they're all just what we expect to eat at Ted's house.

I first met Ted Reader in the fall of 1984 at George Brown College. He was a tall, cherubic kid from Paris, Ontario, with twinkling eyes and a way with the ladies. At first glance it was very easy to write him off as a typical college wise-ass. But second looks are very telling. This boy could cook. Boy, could he cook.

Over the years Ted has worked for me, I have worked for him, and we have collaborated. No matter the relationship, Ted's passion drives any venture. We knew when we saw that first episode of the television show *Cottage Country*—in which Ted appeared as the resident chef—that he had found his medium. Ted is about sharing, and this book is another leap forward in his quest to see the world become as passionate about food and drink as he is.

Over the past few months I have been able to count on a phone call nearly every Thursday or Friday. "What are ya doing Saturday? Come for dinner." Only a fool says no to an invitation to dinner at Ted and Pamela's. I have happily eaten my way through much of the development of this book. There's nothing quite so pleasant as sitting in his backyard watching him expertly manipulate as many as six barbecues and a smoker, not to mention the Brazilian fire pit, at once, all the while sipping beer and the occasional shot of tequila and entertaining us with his trademark banter.

It has been a great pleasure to watch how this book has fairly flowed from Ted's veins. What stands out is the way his imagination translates into such an approachable style. You might not think of cedar planking brie or wrapping shrimp in beef tenderloin, but read the recipes: you'll quickly notice the instructions make perfect sense. Ted's ideas and your skill, no matter the level, will make for an impressive repertoire.

The input of friends and family is an important part of Ted's style. He is a chef who cooks to please his audience more than himself. He is all about "whaddaya think?" We'd eat a fabulous meal and make comments in the course of the evening. A few weeks later a revised dish would appear: one incorporating our suggestions. Our favourite recipes tend to turn up in Ted's books. He garners ideas from friends, from childhood, from restaurants. They will always have a bit of a Ted twist, but he always gives credit where it is due. Once, a few books back, I got a call at 10:30 p.m: "I need a lamb recipe, whaddaya got?" Some months later, the book, which included my recipe, arrived. Inside, he had credited the recipe with the line "from my friend Wendy," but the recipe itself had been transformed. It was now signature Ted. In *On Fire in the Kitchen* there is a recipe called Wendy's Creamed Peas. I used to make them every year at Christmas from my mother's recipe. But, again, these are Ted's Creamed Peas because, although he revived my mother's recipe, with his additions he has made it his own.

Other of his friends turn up in his books. "Mike" is Mike McColl, Ted's right hand and a quiet, funny, terribly talented chef. On New Year's Eve we ate his Spicy Seafood Goodness. I don't think anyone ate less than three helpings. Even Mike's Mom's recipe makes an appearance. Who can resist her pork chops and scalloped potatoes?

To meet Ted's mother is to understand so much about Ted. Her cooking is legendary, her hospitality completely endearing. When we catered her fiftieth wedding anniversary, she was so worried there wouldn't be enough food that we arrived to a mountain of party sandwiches and squares. Her background is Latvian, her borscht to die for. Add a Ted-ly twist and you have nirvana.

Pamela is Ted's reason for being. It's not easy being married to a chef. We are never home at anything approaching normal hours. And we're all a little bit nuts. Somehow, though, Pamela manages to keep it sane. Given the larger-than-life chef in her house, it's amazing that she even tries to cook. But cook she does—and she does it very well. Her spaghetti and meatballs are a lovely nod to a time when everyone's mom made meatballs. At Ted's house these are served in 11-inch pasta show plates, yet they still make me feel like I'm at mom's just the same.

There's local radio star Scruff Connors and Freddy, a nice Italian fella who's also a chef. There's Ted's dad. There's Mrs. Field's relish, she's the mom of his best friend from childhood. Mrs. Jacobson is Pamela's mother and a darn good cook. The Coulson of pickled egg fame is David Coulson, V.P. Sales and Marketing for Napoleon Barbecues. (If you have a secret recipe, don't serve it or even discuss it in Ted's presence.)

Then there are the places that inspire. Ted worked at a resort in Muskoka some years back. The Blueberry White Chocolate Pancakes are insanely decadent and must be tried. The Q107 Breakfast Sandwich came out of a great fall promo he did with the radio station. The Old School is a well-known and very good restaurant that was one of the first places where Ted honed his skills. Their garlic bread is unparalleled.

My favourite example of Ted's far-reaching curiosity is Moon Palace Orange Chicken. Moon Palace is the local take-out place in Ted and Pamela's neighbourhood. Nothing is sacred!

I'm back in time, at my training at George Brown College. It's 4:00 a.m. We're taking part in a culinary competition and none of us has slept for 36 hours or more. We're all shaking intermittently and the girls are prone to sudden crying jags. In a corner a big baby-faced kid is bent over a silver tray carefully positioning perfect little cornucopias of parisienne vegetables on a film of aspic with absolutely steady hands. His control is awesome. He looks up after the last one is in place, shoots me a big stupid grin, and says, "Wanna beer?"

That's Ted.

Wendy Baskerville
April 2004

Introduction

The last twelve months have been eventful. I published a book in the United States, filmed the second season of *King of the Q* on location in the Caribbean, appeared on *Regis and Kelly,* married the lovely Pamela, built a Brazilian churrasco firepit in my backyard, travelled the length and breadth of North America, and even turned forty without my well-meaning friends noticing. It was a *serious* year.

Through all this frenzied activity I somehow managed to write *On Fire in the Kitchen,* too. This cookbook embraces my life in food: or rather, the food in my life. For those of you who don't know me, everything I do—particularly when it relates to food—I do big and with passion. But it's the people around me who are the fuel that drives my passion—the passion to see every man, woman and child smacking their lips with the satisfaction only a homemade meal can provide. For that reason, there's much of me—as well as my wife, my family, my friends and my colleagues—in these recipes.

As I "prepped" this book, Pamela and I enfolded friends and family around us and cooked. It often began in the hot tub! Pamela and I have been known to spend a lot of our down time (not that we get that much down time) playing crib before or after a good soak. Conversation during these moments inevitably turns to new and inventive ways to prepare food and, in no time, we are on the phone to friends, inviting them over to help cook up crazy and delicious feasts. Pamela was on appetizers and desserts duty most of the time. Sometimes the chores were dished out farther afield—Mom often brought dessert, my friend Wendy brought soup, Mike made lunch and it was The Full Monty (Cristo). We ate and laughed and drank and talked and loved being together.

And nothing was sacred. So there's Spam crouton's in bean soup on page 79 and there's my BBQ Chicken Sundae on page 29. Then there's my meat loaf surprise. The rather unusual and long title for this recipe (page 139) was inspired by the reaction of a neighbour at the sight of his serving.

This book begins with soups and salads. Pamela loves salads, and the simpler the better. For her, there's nothing more satisfying than a big wedge of iceberg lettuce served with my Caramelized Onion and Oka Cheese Ranch Dressing (page 88). Both she and I are partial to Pucker Up and Smack Me Lemon Vinaigrette (page 91), too. Why? Well, because it calls for lots of fresh lemon juice, which makes the salad so good you'll forget the rest of the meal and just pucker up!

What is it about some dishes that only moms can do right, like Warm Carrot Salad (page 102)? My mom brought it to the family dinner the night before our wedding. It certainly made us feel warm and fuzzy to have this Reader family classic on the buffet table on that special night. When we go to the Jacobsons' house for a barbecue, inevitably I end up grilling the whole shebang. Except for the potato salad. Mrs. J. does a goody. It's another mom thing!

On the subject of barbecues, I made the Cedar-Planked Brie with Pineapple Topping (page 55) for a little backyard grill one summer Saturday night and somebody said that it was so good it was better than sex. Now, you know you've got to try that one! I feel much the same about the Grilled Texas Shrimp Wrapped in Beef Tenderloin (page 62). I made that for Henry Waszczuk when I guested on the OLN TV show *Fishing the Flats* with him not so long ago. When making this, I like to buy thinly sliced beef, like the kind you can get in Korean markets, and really big, juicy tiger shrimp. The beef gets all crispy and the shrimp are *only just* cooked. The silence and sighs that result when everyone starts eating is pure delight.

When it comes to side dishes, I look to inject fun and creativity whenever possible. Instead of potato, for instance, use yucca. I love yucca, a South American relative of potatoes and available in most supermarkets. I can eat yucca till I turn purple. Pamela loves my Yucca Hash (page 207) with lots of caramelized onion and bits of bacon. If you have a hankering for more traditional fare, there's always Scalloped Potatoes and Sweet Corn (page 211). It truly is heaven in a pan. I'm proud to say there are never any leftovers at my dinner parties when this is served.

Lots of people claim to be the originator of drunken (or beer can) chicken. I'm not and don't claim to be—but boy do I ever promote this method of cooking. It's just so much fun going through the steps and so satisfying to end up with a succulent, yummy bird. I'm such a devotee of drunken chicken that, for this book, I created a his-and-hers version. His is the usual yummy beer-infused bird while the more elegant (hers) version is infused with white wine, fresh lemon, and herbs—delicate but so good you'll want to rip the chicken apart with your hands.

When it comes time to consider dessert, make it decadent or don't bother. But decadent doesn't necessarily mean difficult: instead, it can be as simple as my take on Warm Rice Pudding with Grilled Pineapple, Macadamia Nuts and Rum Syrup (page 228). It's a classic and there's always a battle over who gets the last serving.

Because cooking and grilling and shaking and baking is fun, this ultimately is a book about having fun, whether you have four or twelve people to dinner. If the table's not set, don't freak! Just enlist your sister's help. If the cream needs whipping, then hand it off to her husband. Need the lettuce torn and tossed? A neighbour can do it. It's my experience that when everybody is involved in preparing a meal, conversation and hilarity ensue. And for a little while nothing matters but being there with friends and family and lots of good food.

Oh, and lot's of beer. So ... have a beer, peel an onion, chop a mango, sip some beer, throw some stuff in a bowl, sip some more beer, laugh with your friends, sip that beer again. Suddenly there's salsa in the bowl. (If it feels like work you're not doing it right.) And don't forget to be imaginative with every aspect of the meal, even when serving. I've been known, for instance, to use a Tonka truck when serving french fries: it's a cheap and easy way to elicit laughs, and admiration, too.

Start cooking, have fun, go crazy, and relax. I've given you some of my best tricks: the maps are laid out. Yukon Jack Beef Ribs with Gold Rush Honey Garlic Sauce (page 130) only sounds complicated. Sit down and read it: you'll see there is no mystery here, just lovin' and rubbin' and gettin' sticky together.

Ted Reader
April 2004

Scrump-did-lee-icious
breakfast treats

Oven-Baked Carb-Free Frittata

This is a fast and easy carbohydrate-free frittata. It's deliciously easy. But don't ya just wish you could have some toast with butter!

8 slices bacon, cut into 1-inch pieces
6 white mushrooms, cut into eighths
1 medium red bell pepper, thinly sliced
1 jalapeño pepper, diced
1 cup diced smoked ham
2 tbsp. chopped fresh herbs
8 eggs
1/4 cup heavy cream
1 cup shredded two-year-old white Canadian Cheddar cheese
3 tbsp. grated Parmesan cheese
Salt and pepper

1. Preheat oven to 350°F. Lightly spray a 9-inch glass pie plate with nonstick cooking spray.
2. In a frying pan over medium-high heat, sauté the bacon until halfway to crisp. Add the mushrooms and continue to sauté, stirring until mushrooms are tender and brown. Remove from heat and add the bell pepper, jalapeño pepper, ham and herbs. Let cool slightly.
3. Crack the eggs into a large bowl. Add the cream and beat the eggs. Stir in Cheddar, Parmesan and the bacon mixture. Season to taste with salt and pepper. Pour the egg mixture into the pie plate. Bake 25 to 30 minutes, until the egg is set.
4. Remove frittata from the pan and let rest for 5 minutes. Cut into 6 wedges and serve with your choice of salad.

Serves 6

The "Service Stopper" Lobster Omelette with Lemon Sour Cream

My chef, Mike McColl, made the mistake of offering this omelette as a special one day at Rodney's Oyster House in Toronto. He got so many orders that he was too busy to cook anything else.

Fresh lobster is best, but you can use thawed frozen in a pinch.

Lemon Sour Cream

1/2 cup sour cream

2 tbsp. lemon juice

1 tsp. finely grated lemon zest

1 tsp. chopped fresh dill

Salt and pepper

1/2 small Brie wheel (130 g)

12 spears asparagus

4 eggs

1/4 cup heavy cream

2 tbsp. butter

1/2 cup diced red onion

1 lb. cooked lobster meat, cut into 1/2-inch chunks

Salt and pepper

1. To make the Lemon Sour Cream, whisk together the sour cream, lemon juice, lemon zest and dill. Season to taste with salt and pepper. Refrigerate until needed.
2. Slice the Brie into 1/4-inch strips. Cut the asparagus diagonally into 1/4-inch slices (you should have about 1 cup). Whisk together the eggs and the cream.
3. Melt 1 tbsp. of the butter in an 8- to 10-inch nonstick frying pan over medium heat. Add the onion and asparagus; sauté until the asparagus is crisp-tender, about 5 minutes. Add the lobster; sauté until heated through, 1 to 2 minutes. Transfer the lobster mixture to a bowl.
4. Reduce the heat to medium-low and return the pan to the stove. Melt the remaining 1 tbsp. of butter. Pour in the egg mixture. Stir very gently until the egg is halfway cooked and then stop stirring. Cook the omelette another 2 to 3 minutes or until nearly cooked through. Spoon the lobster mixture along the centre of the omelette. Top with the Brie. Attempt to roll the whole mess onto a plate.
5. Serve with Lemon Sour Cream.

Serves 2

Cheesy Biscuits with Sausage Cream Gravy

Biscuits and gravy is a southern breakfast classic. I used to make this at every race on the CART racing circuit. After a few biscuits and a ladle or two of sausage gravy, ya'd better take a big nap.

Sausage Cream Gravy

2 lb. sausage meat

1 tbsp. Bone Dust BBQ Spice (see page 42)

1 tbsp. vegetable oil

2 tbsp. butter

1/4 cup flour

1 cup milk

1 cup heavy cream

1 tbsp. chopped fresh sage

1 tsp. dry mustard

1/2 tsp. salt

1/2 tsp. black pepper

Worcestershire sauce and hot sauce to taste

Cheesy Biscuits

2 1/2 cups sifted all-purpose flour

1 tbsp. baking powder

1 tsp. salt

1/2 cup butter

3/4 cup buttermilk

1 cup shredded Cheddar or Swiss cheese

1 tbsp. chopped fresh herbs (such as thyme, sage or parsley)

Pinch black pepper

Pinch cayenne pepper

1. To make the gravy, in a bowl, combine the sausage meat and Bone Dust BBQ Spice. In a large, deep frying pan, heat the oil over high heat. Fry the sausage meat in small batches until fully cooked. Transfer with a slotted spoon to paper towels to drain. Reserve excess fat.

2. Using a wooden spoon, scrape loose the little bits of cooked sausage meat from the bottom of the pan. Return the pan to medium heat and melt the butter in 2 tbsp. of the reserved fat. Add the flour, stirring until it is completely blended with the butter mixture. Add the milk 1/2 cup at a time, stirring constantly until the mixture has no flour lumps. Add the cream and continue stirring until fully mixed and smooth. Add reserved sausage meat and bring mixture to a low boil. Reduce heat to low and simmer, uncovered and stirring occasionally, for 30 minutes or until gravy is thick and smooth and has a nice sausage flavour. Season with fresh herbs, mustard, salt, pepper, Worcestershire sauce and hot sauce.

3. While gravy is simmering, make the biscuits. Preheat oven to 425°F. Line a baking sheet with parchment paper and lightly grease the paper.

4. Sift the flour, baking powder and salt into a bowl. Using your fingers or a pastry blender, blend in the butter until the mixture looks like coarse cornmeal. Add the buttermilk, cheese and herbs; stir until the dough is soft but not gluey and sticky.

5. Dump dough out onto a floured work surface and knead 15 to 20 times. Roll or press the dough out to a thickness of 1 1/2 inches. Cut with a 3-inch biscuit cutter. Reroll the scraps if necessary to make 12 biscuits. Place biscuits on the baking sheet and bake until golden brown, 12 to 15 minutes.

6. Let biscuits cool slightly. Serve warm, topped with Sausage Cream Gravy.

Serves 6

Muskoka Blueberry White Chocolate Pancakes with Blueberry Syrup

Muskoka is Canada's premier cottage country. Notables such as Kurt Russell, Goldie Hawn, Eddie Van Halen and Eric Lindros all own prime real estate there. Besides the celebs, the big-ass cottages, the fast boats, fantastic lakes and the odd mosquito, the Muskokas have great wild blueberries. I made these pancakes while working at a fishing and hunting lodge back in the 80s. Wicked!

2 large eggs, well beaten

1 1/2 cups buttermilk

1/4 cup melted shortening or butter

2 1/4 cups all-purpose flour

1 tbsp. sugar

1 tbsp. baking powder

1/2 tsp. salt

8 tbsp. butter

1 1/2 cups fresh or frozen blueberries

1 cup white chocolate chips

1. Preheat oven to 200°F. In a bowl, beat the eggs well. Whisk in the buttermilk and shortening. In a large bowl, sift together the flour, sugar, baking powder and salt. Whisk in the egg mixture until just smooth.

2. In a medium nonstick frying pan over medium-high heat, melt 1 to 2 tbsp. of the butter. Using a small ladle, spoon the pancake batter into the hot pan, making three or four pancakes at a time. Sprinkle pancakes with blueberries and chocolate chips. Cook until the bubbles that form on the top of the pancakes begin to burst. Flip and continue to cook until pancakes are golden brown on the bottom, about 1 to 2 more minutes. Transfer pancakes to a baking sheet and keep warm in the oven. Repeat until all the batter is used.

3. Stack pancakes on plates and top with a healthy dollop of butter. Drizzle with warm Blueberry Syrup (recipe follows).

Makes about 12 good-sized pancakes

Blueberry Syrup

1 cup fresh or frozen blueberries

2 cups maple syrup

In a medium saucepan, lightly mash the blueberries. Stir in the maple syrup. Bring to a low boil and simmer for 2 minutes. Remove from heat and let steep for 24 hours. Strain through cheesecloth. Keeps for 3 weeks in the refrigerator. (To reheat syrup, microwave at High for 15 to 20 seconds.)

Makes about 2 cups

Eggs Corona

Here's a winner: poached eggs on warm flour tortillas with refried beans, chorizo sausage, caramelized salsa onions, topped off with a Corona Beer Cheese Sauce. I prepared this breakfast dish for our Team Corona Pit Crew while working on the CART racing circuit for Walker Racing. The key to this recipe is using Corona beer in the cheese sauce. Yes, beer for breakfast. It's a good thing!

Corona Beer Cheese Sauce

2 tbsp. butter

1/4 cup all-purpose flour

1 bottle Corona beer

1 cup water

1 cup cubed Velveeta cheese

1 cup shredded pepper Jack cheese

1 tsp. Worcestershire sauce

1/2 tsp. hot sauce

Cayenne pepper, salt and black pepper to taste

1. In a medium saucepan over medium heat, melt the butter. Stir in the flour and cook, stirring constantly, for 1 to 2 minutes or until the flour mixture is fully mixed and golden.

2. Add the beer and water 1/2 cup at a time, stirring constantly until mixture is smooth and comes to a slow boil. (If the mixture gets too thick, add a little extra beer.) Reduce heat to low and simmer, stirring frequently, for 10 minutes.

3. Remove from heat and stir in the Velveeta cheese and pepper Jack cheese, stirring until the cheeses are fully incorporated and melted. The sauce should be smooth and velvety. Season with Worcestershire sauce, hot sauce, cayenne, salt and pepper.

4. Press a piece of wax or parchment paper onto the surface of the sauce to prevent a skin from forming. Set aside and keep warm.

Salsa Onions

2 tbsp. vegetable oil

1 clove garlic, minced

1 large sweet onion, thinly sliced

1 jalapeño pepper, finely chopped

1 ripe tomato, diced

Juice of 1 lime

1 tbsp. chopped fresh cilantro

Salt and black pepper

1. Heat the oil in a large frying pan over medium heat. Sauté the garlic and onion, stirring constantly, for 8 to 10 minutes, until the onions are tender and golden brown.
2. Stir in the jalapeño and tomatoes and cook, stirring, until the tomatoes are just soft. Add lime juice, cilantro, and salt and black pepper to taste. Remove from heat and keep warm.

Guacamole

1 ripe avocado, seeded and mashed

Juice of 1 lime

1 tbsp. chopped fresh cilantro

1 tbsp. vegetable oil

Salt and pepper

In a bowl, mash the avocado with a fork. Stir in the lime juice, cilantro and oil. Season to taste with salt and pepper. Cover surface with plastic wrap and set aside.

The Final Assembly

4 smoked chorizo or other smoked sausage (about 3 oz. each)

2 tbsp. white vinegar

4 to 8 large eggs

4 7-inch flour tortillas

1 cup refried beans

Salt and pepper

1 cup shredded pepper Jack cheese

4 sprigs fresh cilantro

1. Preheat oven to 375°F.
2. Place the chorizo sausage in a roasting pan and roast for 15 to 20 minutes, until lightly browned and crisp. Cover loosely with foil and set aside. Keep the oven on.
3. Pour a few inches of water into a medium saucepan. Add the vinegar. Bring to a rolling boil, then reduce heat so the water just simmers. Using a slotted spoon, gently stir the water clockwise so that the water is slightly swirling.
4. Crack eggs one at a time into the barely simmering water. Poach eggs until whites are set and yolks are still soft, about 4 minutes. Using a slotted spoon, remove poached eggs from pot and drain on paper towels. Set aside, keeping warm.
5. Warm flour tortillas directly on oven rack for 2 to 3 minutes or until soft and warm.
6. Meanwhile, in a microwave-safe bowl, stir the refried beans until smooth. Season to taste with salt and pepper. Microwave the beans at High for 1 to 2 minutes or until warm.
7. Put one tortilla on each plate. Spread 2 tbsp. of the beans on each tortilla, spreading beans to the edge. Diagonally slice the chorizo sausages and lay slices over the beans. Top with Salsa Onions (see page 13). Place poached eggs on the onions. Ladle 1/3 cup of Corona Beer Cheese Sauce (see page 12) over the eggs. Sprinkle each serving with 1/4 cup pepper Jack cheese.
8. Serve immediately, garnished with a dollop of Guacamole (see page 13) and a sprig of cilantro.

Serves 4

The Q107 Breakfast Sandwich

For nine weeks, every Friday, my chef, Mike McColl, and I had the great pleasure of cooking at a different radio Q107 listener's home for the Q107 "Derringer's Tour of the Neighbourhood." Twenty to fifty guests each Friday! A different home, a different kitchen, a lot of food and beer. Up at 4—that's a.m., folks—and cooking at 5. Eating till 9. For all you Q107 fans, this is our "Classic Rock with Derringer in the Morning" breakfast sandwich.

1/4 cup maple syrup

1/4 cup beer

1/4 cup BBQ sauce

1 tbsp. Bone Dust BBQ Spice (see page 42)

2 lb. sliced peameal bacon

4 burger buns

1 cup shredded Cheddar or mozzarella cheese

1. Preheat grill to medium-high.
2. In a bowl, stir together the maple syrup, beer and BBQ sauce.
3. Grill the peameal bacon, basting liberally with the maple sauce, for 2 minutes per side. Stack the bacon into four piles. Mound 1/4 cup of cheese on each stack and let the cheese melt.
4. Lightly toast both sides of the burger buns on the grill. Place burger-bun bottoms on each of four plates. Place a bacon-and-melted-cheese stack on each bun, followed by a lid. Serve with a daily dose of Derringer.

Serves 4

Tip: For an added twist, top peameal with scrambled eggs.

Injected Carrot Nut Creamsicle Muffins

I believe the only good muffin is an injected muffin. Tim Hortons has their exploding-fruit muffins, and I have created the Cheez Whiz–injected bacon Cheddar muffins. Now, make way for Injected Carrot Nut Creamsicle Muffins!

2 cups all-purpose flour

2 tbsp. brown sugar

1 tbsp. baking powder

1/2 tsp. salt

1 large egg

1 cup heavy cream

1/4 cup + 3 tbsp. melted butter

1/2 cup chopped walnuts

1 cup grated carrots

Cream Cheese Creamsicle Icing

1/2 cup cream cheese, softened

1/4 cup sifted icing sugar

2 to 3 tbsp. fresh orange juice

1/2 tsp. orange zest

Seeds from 1/4 of a vanilla pod

1. Preheat oven to 425°F. Grease a muffin pan.
2. In a large bowl, sift together the flour, brown sugar, baking powder and salt.
3. In a medium bowl, beat the egg well. Stir in the cream and melted butter. Add the wet ingredients to the dry ingredients and stir well until the mixture is thoroughly combined. Stir in the walnuts and carrots.
4. Spoon the batter into the muffin tins, filling each one three-quarters full. Bake 20 to 25 minutes or until the muffins are nicely browned and a toothpick inserted in the middle of a muffin comes out clean. Remove muffins from pan and let cool on a rack.
5. To make the icing, in a medium bowl, beat together the cream cheese, icing sugar, orange juice, zest and vanilla seeds until light and fluffy.
6. Fit a pastry bag with a #5 tip. Fill pastry bag with cream cheese mixture. Insert piping tip into centre of carrot muffins and squeeze. Pull out and drizzle extra icing over the muffin.

Makes 1 dozen muffins

Bahamian-Style Chicken Souse with Poached Eggs

While filming *King of the Q* in the Bahamas in 2002, we had a breakfast that rocked. It was a chicken souse, essentially chicken stewed in a broth and served with a poached egg. Wonderfully seasoned, spicy and tender chicken is a perfect start to the day, especially with a cold beer. In the Bahamas they leave in the thyme sprigs and bay leaf, but you can take them out before serving if you're not in a rustic mood.

4 chicken legs, scored to expose some bone

2 chicken breasts

3 large Yukon Gold potatoes, peeled and cut into 1-inch pieces

4 medium red onions, cut into 1-inch pieces

2 medium leeks, washed well and cut into 1/2-inch rounds

2 medium carrots, cut into 1/2-inch rounds

12 peppercorns

4 whole allspice

1 bay leaf

1 whole clove

Pinch grated nutmeg

2 sprigs fresh thyme

1 tsp. salt

Black pepper to taste

2 tbsp. white vinegar

4 large eggs

2 limes, halved

1. In a 4- to 5-quart pot, combine the chicken pieces, potatoes, onions, leeks, carrots, peppercorns, allspice, bay leaf, clove, nutmeg, thyme and salt. Cover with water and bring to a boil over high heat without stirring.

2. Skim the froth that accumulates at the top and stir once. Return to the boil and skim the froth again. Reduce the heat to medium-low and simmer, uncovered and without stirring, for 1 1/2 hours or until the chicken is very tender and fully cooked.

3. Remove the chicken pieces from the pot and let cool slightly. Pull the meat from the bones and return meat to the broth. Discard bones. Increase heat to medium and simmer souse for 15 minutes. Season with salt and pepper.

4. Meanwhile, pour a few inches of water into a medium saucepan. Add the vinegar. Bring to a rolling boil, then reduce heat so the water just simmers. Using a slotted spoon, gently stir the water clockwise so that the water is slightly swirling.

5. Crack eggs one at a time into the barely simmering water. Poach eggs until whites are set and yolks are still soft, about 4 minutes. Using a slotted spoon, remove poached eggs from pot and drain on paper towels.

6. Place a poached egg in each soup bowl. Spoon the souse over the eggs, making sure each bowl receives an ample serving of chicken and vegetables. Serve immediately, garnished with a lime half.

Serves 4

Build 'em and stack 'em sandwiches

Surf and Turf Burgers

When you want a fancied-up burger, try this one — pure burger decadence. Ground sirloin of beef stuffed with fresh lobster meat and aged Cheddar cheese. Truly a drool-able experience.

1/2 cup cream cheese, softened

1 cup fresh or well-drained thawed frozen lobster meat

1/2 cup shredded aged white Cheddar cheese

2 tsp. chopped fresh dill

1 tsp. lemon juice

Salt and pepper

1 1/2 lb. ground sirloin

1 small onion, diced

2 cloves garlic, minced

1 tbsp. Dijon mustard

1 to 2 tbsp. Bone Dust BBQ Spice (see page 42)

3 to 4 tsp. Worcestershire sauce

3/4 cup clarified butter (see page 208)

1/4 cup ketchup

1 tbsp. chopped fresh herbs (such as parsley, dill or chives)

2 tsp. Worcestershire sauce

6 lobster claws

6 hamburger buns

1/4 cup mayonnaise

6 leaves leaf lettuce

1 small onion, thinly sliced

2 ripe tomatoes, thinly sliced

1. In a food processor, process cream cheese until smooth. Add lobster, Cheddar cheese, dill, and lemon juice, and salt and pepper to taste. Pulse until mixed. Shape mixture into patties about 2 inches wide and 1/2 inch thick. Place on a plate lined with wax paper and refrigerate, covered, while you prepare the burgers.

2. In a bowl, combine the sirloin, onion, garlic and mustard. Season to taste with Bone Dust BBQ Spice and 1 to 2 tsp. of the Worcestershire sauce. Mix until well combined. Shape into 12 patties 3 to 4 inches wide, pressing each patty firmly so it holds together. Place burgers on a tray lined with wax paper and refrigerate, covered, for 30 minutes.

3. Top six sirloin burgers with the lobster patties. Top with remaining sirloin burgers, crimping and pressing the edges to form a tight seal around the lobster. Freeze burgers on a tray lined with wax paper for 30 minutes to get everything really cold and to let the meat rest before cooking.

4. Preheat grill to medium-high.

5. Meanwhile, in a small saucepan over low heat, stir together the clarified butter, ketchup, herbs and remaining 2 tsp. Worcestershire sauce. Heat until warm. Remove from heat and keep warm.

6. Grill burgers for 4 to 6 minutes on one side. Turn over, baste with butter sauce and cook for 3 to 5 more minutes, until the beef is just cooked and the lobster centre is warm and creamy.

7. While the burgers are cooking, brush the lobster claws with the butter sauce and grill for 1 to 2 minutes, turning once, until lightly charred and heated through.

8. Spread the bottom half of each burger bun with mayonnaise. Top with leaf lettuce. Place burger on top and top burgers with a lobster claw and onion and tomato slices. Top with top half of bun.

Serves 6

The Ultimate BBQ Chicken Burger

As a burger lover, I have tried many in my travels, some horrible and some outstanding. In my opinion, this one is the best chicken burger so far. To keep the ground chicken from drying out on the grill, I like to add cheese and then wrap the burger in a flattened chicken breast. You get a moist and tasty burger with a tender bite of chicken breast.

1/2 lb. Monterey Jack cheese

1 lb. ground chicken

1 large egg, lightly beaten

2 green onions, chopped

1/2 cup diced onion

1/4 cup grated Parmesan cheese

2 tbsp. dry bread crumbs

2 tbsp. chopped fresh herbs

3 tbsp. Bone Dust BBQ Spice (see page 42)

6 boneless skinless chicken breasts (each 4 oz.)

1/4 cup honey

1/4 cup BBQ sauce

Splash lemon juice

1 to 2 tbsp. vegetable oil

6 multigrain hamburger buns

1/2 cup Caramelized Onion and Oka Ranch Dressing (see page 88)

1 pint alfalfa or onion sprouts

1 to 2 avocados, sliced

1 to 2 tomatoes, sliced

1. Cut the Monterey Jack into 1/4-inch cubes. Spread cheese on a tray so the cubes are not touching and freeze for 1 hour. (Freezing the cheese makes it melt slowly, so that when the chicken is cooked the cheese is soft.)
2. In a bowl, combine the ground chicken, egg, green onions, Parmesan, bread crumbs, herbs and 1 tbsp. of the Bone Dust BBQ Spice. Mix well. Add the frozen cheese and mix well.
3. Using a 3-oz. ice cream scoop (or your hands), scoop the chicken mixture into six balls. Using your hands, pat the balls to press out excess air. Press each ball into a patty 1/2 inch thick. Place on a tray lined with wax paper and freeze for 15 minutes to help the meat set and rest.

4. Meanwhile, using a sharp knife, cut each chicken breast down one side from top to bottom, cutting almost to the edge but not all the way through. Splay out the meat to butterfly. Place chicken breasts, one at a time, between two sheets of plastic wrap and, using a meat mallet or rolling pin, gently pound the meat to a uniform 1/2-inch thickness, keeping the breast intact. Season both sides of the chicken with the remaining 2 tbsp. Bone Dust BBQ Spice.

5. Top each flattened chicken breast with a burger. Wrap the chicken breast around the patty, completely encasing the burger inside the breast. Wrap burgers in plastic wrap and refrigerate for 1 hour.

6. Meanwhile, preheat grill to high.

7. In a bowl, stir together the honey, BBQ sauce and lemon juice. Set aside.

8. Brush chicken burgers with the oil. Grill for 1 to 2 minutes per side to sear. Reduce heat to low. Close the lid and grill for 10 to 15 minutes, basting frequently with the honey sauce, until the burgers are well done.

9. Place burgers on the bun bottoms and top with Caramelized Onion and Oka Ranch Dressing, alfalfa sprouts and avocado and tomato slices.

Serves 6

Harmony Burger

My friend Jeff Soltysiak took me to a diner in Kitchener-Waterloo, Ontario, called Harmony Lunch, famous for its rich and tasty pork burger (a secret recipe passed from generation to generation) topped with fried onions and served on a lightly toasted bun. Rumour has it that the late Dave Thomas, of Wendy's fame, tried to buy the recipe. This is the closest I can get to re-creating it.

1 lb. finely ground pork	1/2 tsp. cayenne pepper
1 lb. coarsely ground pork	4 cloves garlic
1/2 cup dry white bread crumbs	1 small onion, cut in chunks
2 large egg whites	4 tbsp. vegetable shortening
1 tbsp. salt	2 large onions, thinly sliced
2 tsp. white pepper	Salt and black pepper
1 tbsp. dry mustard	6 to 8 white hamburger buns
1 tbsp. Bone Dust BBQ Spice (see page 42)	Mustard, relish and sliced cheese, for garnish

1. Put the ground pork, bread crumbs, egg whites, salt, white pepper, dry mustard, Bone Dust BBQ Spice and cayenne pepper in the bowl of a stand mixer.
2. In a food processor, process the garlic and onion chunks until smooth. Add to the pork mixture. Beat pork mixture on low speed for 1 to 2 minutes, until smooth. Beat on medium-high for 10 seconds. Cover and refrigerate for 1 hour.
3. Using a 3- to 4-oz. ice cream scoop (or your hands), scoop the pork into balls, pressing the meat to pack it firmly. Unmould balls onto a tray and set aside.
4. Preheat oven to 200°F.
5. In a large frying pan, melt 1 tbsp. of the shortening over medium-high heat. Add the sliced onions and sauté, stirring, for 15 to 20 minutes, until onions are tender and golden brown. Season to taste with salt and black pepper. Transfer onions to a bowl.
6. In the same pan, melt 1/2 tsp. of the shortening per burger over medium-high heat. Place one harmony scoop, flat side down, in the pan and flatten it with a spatula to a thickness of 1/2 inch. Repeat with two to three more burgers. Fry burgers for 2 to 3 minutes per side, until cooked through. Transfer cooked burgers to a baking sheet and keep warm in the oven. Repeat with remaining scoops.
7. Put burgers on warmed burger buns and top with fried onions. Serve with mustard, relish and your choice of cheese, if you wish.

Serves 6 to 8

Fall Fair Horn Dog Corn Dogs with Wasabi Mustard Dippin' Sauce

This recipe—a tribute to the corn dogs that were never available at my fall fair in Paris, Ontario, when I was a kid—involves deep-frying, so please be careful.

Wasabi Mustard Dippin' Sauce

1/4 cup prepared mustard

1 tsp. wasabi powder

1/4 cup honey

1 tbsp. grainy mustard

1 tbsp. lemon juice

1 1/2 cups all-purpose flour

3/4 cup fine cornmeal

1/4 cup grated Parmesan cheese

3 tbsp. sugar

2 tsp. baking powder

1 tsp. salt

3 tbsp. melted butter

2 large eggs, beaten

1 1/2 cups buttermilk

8 jumbo hot dogs (pork, all beef, chicken or turkey)

8 cups vegetable oil

1. To make the Wasabi Mustard Dippin' Sauce, in a bowl, whisk together the prepared mustard and wasabi until smooth. Add the honey, grainy mustard and lemon juice; whisk until blended. Set aside.
2. Sift the flour into a large bowl. Add the cornmeal, Parmesan cheese, sugar, baking powder and salt; stir to combine. Using a fork, stir in the melted butter. Whisk together the eggs and buttermilk. Add to flour mixture until just incorporated. Let batter stand for 15 minutes.
3. Meanwhile, pat hot dogs dry. Push a wooden chopstick or thick wood or bamboo skewer about 3/4 of the way into each dog.
4. Preheat oven to 200°F. Preheat countertop deep-fryer to 365°F (or heat oil to 375°F in a large, heavy pot).
5. Using the stick as a handle, dip each hot dog into the batter to fully coat the dog. Holding the stick, immediately dip the coated dog into the oil and slowly turn the dog in the oil. When it starts to bubble, let go. Cook for 6 to 8 minutes, turning frequently, until golden brown on all sides. Transfer corn dog to a baking sheet lined with paper towels to drain and keep warm in the oven. Repeat with remaining dogs.
6. Serve with Wasabi Mustard Dippin' Sauce.

Serves 4

Scruff's Baked Potato Tuna Melt

Q107 Radio, which can be heard in Toronto and other parts of Southern Ontario, is classic rock at its best. One of the "Q" DJ pioneers is Scruff Connors. I have been a loyal fan since I first heard Scruff in 1978. Years later, Scruff and I met, and now we drink beer and talk food a lot. Here is a dish that Scruff loves to make. It's not really a sandwich, but that's how he refers to his recipe. Enjoy!

2 very large baking potatoes (each 8 to 12 oz.), scrubbed

1 can tuna in water, drained

1/4 cup finely diced onion

1/2 stalk celery, finely chopped

2 green onions, chopped

1 tsp. Bone Dust BBQ Spice (see page 42)

1 tsp. dry mustard

Pinch cayenne pepper

Squeeze fresh lemon juice

1/4 to 1/3 cup mayonnaise or ranch dressing

Salt and black pepper

1/2 cup shredded Cheddar cheese

1/2 cup shredded mozzarella cheese

1. Preheat oven to 425°F.
2. Bake potatoes for 60 to 75 minutes, until fully cooked and tender. Remove from oven and microwave at High for 30 seconds. (This helps to dry out the inside of the potatoes, which makes them lighter and fluffier.) Do not turn off the oven.
3. While the potatoes are baking, prepare the tuna salad. In a medium bowl, combine the tuna, onion, celery, green onions, Bone Dust BBQ Spice, mustard, cayenne, lemon juice and mayonnaise. Using a fork, mix thoroughly. The tuna should be moist and spreadable, not dry and crumbly. Season to taste with salt and black pepper. Set aside.
4. Cut the baked potatoes in half lengthwise. Carefully scoop out the flesh, being careful not to break the skins. Put the skins on a baking sheet. Add the potato flesh to the tuna salad. Add the Cheddar and mozzarella cheese. Stir to combine. Season to taste with salt and pepper. Spoon tuna mixture into potato skins, piling it high. Bake for 8 to 12 minutes, until heated through and cheese is melting and oozing. Serve with a fork and spoon.

Serves 6

Spank da Plank Salmon Salad Sandwich

This sandwich is best made with leftover Cedar-Planked Salmon (see page 190). Sometimes there aren't any leftovers, so make it fresh. Hot, smoked, tender and moist salmon: a vast improvement on plain and simple canned salmon.

4 skinless salmon fillets (each 5 oz.)

1 tbsp. Bone Dust BBQ Spice (see page 42)

1/2 cup diced red onion

2 tbsp. chopped fresh dill

2 tbsp. lemon juice

1 green onion, chopped

2 tbsp. olive oil

1/2 cup shredded Havarti cheese

1/4 cup mayonnaise

1 tsp. Dijon mustard

Salt and pepper

4 tbsp. butter

4 hamburger buns, halved

4 leaves green leaf lettuce

1 to 2 ripe tomatoes, sliced

8 slices bacon, cooked crisp and kept warm

4 lemon wedges, for garnish

Special equipment: 1 untreated cedar plank
        (at least 6 × 12 inches and 1/2-inch thick),
        soaked in cold water for at least 1 hour

1. Preheat grill to high.
2. Rub the salmon with the Bone Dust BBQ Spice, pressing the seasoning into the flesh. Place the salmon on the plank.
3. In a bowl, stir together the red onion, dill, lemon juice, green onion and olive oil. Top the salmon with this mixture.
4. Place the plank on the grill and close the lid. Grill for 15 to 20 minutes until hot and cooked through. Remove the plank from the grill and let salmon cool for 10 minutes.
5. Transfer the salmon to a bowl and mash it with a fork. Add the Havarti, mayonnaise and mustard; gently mix to bind. Season to taste with salt and pepper.
6. In a large frying pan over medium-high heat, melt 2 tbsp. of the butter. Brown the bottoms of the hamburger buns, cut sides down, until golden brown and crisp. Repeat with tops of buns. Garnish bottom half of each bun with lettuce and tomato. Top with a generous scoop of salmon salad and 2 slices of bacon. Top with bun and serve with a lemon wedge and a squeeze.

Serves 4

Sort of a Catfish Poorboy Sandwich

Whenever I'm in the southern U.S.A. and especially in New Orleans, I like to have a po'boy sandwich. This is a hollowed-out torpedo roll filled with lettuce, mayo, sometimes tomato and breaded fried oysters, shrimp, crawfish and other species of seafood. The following is my version.

2 to 3 large firm ripe red or green tomatoes	4 catfish fillets (each 4 oz.)
1 cup all-purpose flour	3 tbsp. butter
2 tbsp. Bayou Bite Cajun Rub (see page 44)	4 tbsp. vegetable oil
2 large eggs	2 cups shredded iceberg lettuce
1/4 cup store-bought ranch dressing	1 small red onion, very thinly sliced
2 cups dry bread crumbs	8 slices white bread
1 cup grated Parmesan cheese	1 cup Smoky Bacon Blue Cheese Dip (see page 53)
1/2 cup fine cornmeal	Bread-and-butter pickles and hot sauce, for garnish

1. Core and trim the top and bottom of the tomatoes. Slice the tomatoes into 3/4-inch-thick slices. Lay flat on paper towels to drain slightly.
2. In a shallow bowl, stir together the flour and 1 tbsp. of the Bayou Bite Cajun Rub. In a second shallow bowl, lightly beat the eggs and ranch dressing. In a third shallow bowl, stir together the bread crumbs, Parmesan and cornmeal.
3. Season catfish with remaining 1 tbsp. Cajun seasoning.
4. Dredge the tomatoes, one slice at a time, in the seasoned flour. Dip tomato into the egg, letting excess drip off. Roll gently in bread crumb mixture, pressing gently so the coating adheres. Set tomato slices aside on wax paper. Repeat with the catfish.
5. In a large, heavy frying pan over medium-high heat, melt 2 tbsp. of the butter in 2 tbsp. of the oil. When the butter bubbles, fry the tomato slices, three or four at a time, for 2 to 3 minutes per side, turning once, until golden brown. Drain on paper towels. Add remaining oil and butter to the pan and fry the catfish for 1 to 3 minutes per side, or until golden brown and cooked through. Drain on paper towels.
6. In a small bowl, toss together the lettuce and onion. Toast bread and brush with butter. Top with lettuce mixture. Add a couple of slices of fried tomato. Spread some Bacon Blue Cheese Dip over the tomatoes. Top with catfish. Top with more Bacon Blue Cheese Dip and finish with a slice of toast.
7. Serve with bread-and-butter pickles and hot sauce on the side.

Serves 4

Drunken Chicken BBQ Sundaes

A recipe for leftover drunken chicken. Yeah, right, like you'd ever have leftovers. But just in case, here's a great way to use them.

6 large Yukon Gold potatoes, cubed

2 tbsp. butter

1 cup milk

2 tbsp. Roasted Garlic (see page 221)

Salt and pepper

1/4 cup BBQ sauce

2 cups shredded His Oven-Roasted Drunken Beer Can Chicken (see page 162)

Bone Dust BBQ Spice (see page 42)

3 cups Banditos Baked Beans (see page 223)

1 cup Hickory Sticks

4 marshmallows

4 sprigs fresh rosemary

Special equipment: 4 half-quart preserving jars

1. In a large pot of boiling salted water, cook the potatoes until tender, 15 to 20 minutes. Drain well and return to pot over low heat for 1 minute to dry the potatoes. Mash the potatoes. Beat in the butter, milk and roasted garlic. Season to taste with salt and pepper.
2. Meanwhile, in a saucepan, warm the BBQ sauce. Stir in the shredded chicken. Season to taste with Bone Dust BBQ Spice.
3. Evenly divide the Banditos Baked Beans among the jars. Top with chicken mixture. Evenly divide mashed potatoes among the jars. Top with Hickory Sticks.
4. Skewer each marshmallow with a rosemary sprig. Serve sundaes garnished with skewered toasted marshmallows.

Serves 4

Big-Breasted Club Sandwich with Sub Sauce

Nothing is more satisfying to me than a big-ass sandwich. We're talking layers of tender paper-bag-roasted chicken, Black Forest ham, bacon, three cheeses, lettuce, tomatoes, onions and kick-ass sub sauce. Aaahhh.

2 tbsp. balsamic vinegar

2 tbsp. olive oil

2 tbsp. gourmet-style BBQ sauce

1 tsp. Bone Dust BBQ Spice (see page 42)

1 1/2 tsp. crumbled dried oregano

1 baguette

2 cups shredded iceberg lettuce

4 lb. cooked Chicken in a Bag (see page 171; double the recipe), cooled and thinly sliced

6 to 8 slices Provolone cheese

1 lb. shaved Black Forest ham

6 to 8 slices Cheddar cheese

2 large ripe tomatoes, sliced

1 medium red onion, sliced

1 lb. bacon, cooked crisp

6 to 8 slices Swiss cheese

Salt and pepper to taste

1. To make the sub sauce, in a squeeze bottle or small bowl, combine the vinegar, olive oil, BBQ sauce, oregano and Bone Dust BBQ Spice. Shake or stir well. Set aside.

2. Slice the baguette lengthwise, without cutting all the way through. Open up the baguette and pull out the bread in the bottom of the loaf, leaving a canoe-shaped shell. Drizzle the sub sauce evenly over both cut sides of the baguette.

3. Layer the sub as follows:
   - shredded lettuce
   - sliced chicken
   - Provolone cheese
   - ham
   - Cheddar cheese
   - tomatoes
   - red onions
   - bacon
   - Swiss cheese
   - salt and pepper

4. Close the loaf and press down gently on the sub to help stabilize it. Slice into 8 to 10 pieces and serve with condiments galore.

Serves 4 to 8

Leftover Holiday Turkey Sandwich

The leftover turkey sandwich makes it into my Top 10 best-ever sandwiches. Served hot or cold, this baby is what roasting and stuffing a turkey is all about.

4 thick slices bread (traditionally white bread works best but so does sourdough)

2 tsp. butter

A good spread of Dijon mustard

A good spread of mayonnaise

2 leaves leaf lettuce

4 to 6 oz. sliced leftover white turkey meat

Salt and pepper

2 to 4 oz. sliced leftover dark turkey meat

2 tbsp. cranberry sauce

4 oz. leftover turkey stuffing, sliced 1 1/2 inches thick or formed into two 1/2-inch-thick patties

4 slices ripe tomato

4 thin slices red onion

2 slices Swiss cheese

1/2 cup leftover turkey gravy

1. Prepare all your sandwich ingredients. Call out "I've got the La-Z-Boy!" Chill the beer. Put on the fire. Now to make the sandwich …

2. Butter one side of four slices of bread. Spread a nice even amount of Dijon mustard on two slices of buttered bread. Spread a nice even layer of mayonnaise on the other two slices of bread. Top the mayonnaise with lettuce. Top the lettuce with the white meat. Season to taste with salt and pepper. Top the white meat with the dark meat. Season to taste with salt and pepper.

3. Spread on cranberry sauce. Layer with stuffing, tomato, onions and Swiss cheese. Top with Dijon-spread bread slice, mustard side down, of course, otherwise you will mess up the La-Z-Boy. Press down firmly.

4. Cut in half, if you dare. Get beer. Get napkins. Get to your chair. Turn on TV. Take a big bite. Sigh. Smile. Don't forget to chew.

Serves 2

Note: For a hot turkey sandwich, warm the turkey meat and stuffing. Eliminate the lettuce, tomato and onion. Cover with hot turkey gravy, and serve.

Panini of Cambozola Cheese, Bacon and Pear with Gooseberry Relish

Here's a fancy sandwich for when you're feeling like afternoon tea. Instead of eating dainty finger sandwiches, you make this one, a real two-fister. The Queen would be truly mortified.

12 slices thick-cut bacon

4 ciabatta buns (each about 6 inches long), halved lengthwise

2 tsp. Dijon mustard

8 oz. Cambozola cheese, cut into 16 thin slices

1 pear, cored, cut into quarters and thinly sliced

8 leaves fresh basil

Pepper

2 tsp. butter

1. Cook the bacon in a large frying pan until just crisp and most of the fat is rendered. Drain on paper towels.
2. Brush the cut side of the ciabatta buns with mustard and layer with the bacon, Cambozola cheese, pear slices and basil leaves. Season with pepper to taste. Close up the buns. Butter the outsides of the buns.
3. Heat a large, heavy frying pan over medium-low heat. Put sandwiches into the pan. Weigh down with a heavy skillet or a foil-wrapped brick to flatten the sandwich. Turn once or twice until the buns are toasted golden and the Cambozola is melted.
4. Cut each bun in half and serve with Gooseberry Relish.

Serves 4

Gooseberry Relish

1 tsp. butter

1 medium shallot, diced

1 tsp. minced ginger

1 1/2 cups halved fresh gooseberries

1/2 cup Riesling wine

1/4 cup sugar

3 tbsp. cider vinegar

In a medium saucepan over medium-high heat, melt the butter. Sauté the shallot and ginger for 1 to 2 minutes or until tender. Stir in the gooseberries, wine, sugar and vinegar. Bring mixture to a boil, reduce heat and simmer, stirring occasionally, until syrupy and the gooseberries are soft, 5 to 15 minutes. Let cool.

Makes 1 1/2 cups

Roasted Portobello Sandwich with Buffalo Mozzarella, Arugula and Tomato on Toasted Balsamic Garlic Bread

Hey, what happened to this sandwich? Someone stole the meat! Yes, I can do vegetarian cuisine—as long as I can use cheese or eggs and other dairy items. Maybe a little lamb, too?

4 Portobello mushroom caps

Balsamic vinegar

4 cloves garlic, minced

1 tbsp. Amazing Steak Spice (see page 43)

1/4 cup olive oil, plus additional for drizzling

4 thick slices crusty Italian bread (1 inch thick and about 6 inches long)

1 bunch arugula, coarse stems discarded

2 vine-ripened tomatoes, sliced

1 cup very thinly sliced red onion

1 ball buffalo mozzarella, cut into 1/2-inch-thick slices

Cracked black pepper to taste

1. Place mushroom caps in a bowl and cover with hot water. Top with a small plate to keep the mushrooms submerged. Soak mushrooms for 10 to 15 minutes. Drain mushrooms and pat dry with paper towels.

2. Preheat oven to 400°F.

3. In a bowl, whisk together a drizzle of balsamic vinegar, the garlic, Amazing Steak Spice and oil. Place mushroom caps on a baking sheet, gill side up. Fill gills with balsamic marinade. Marinate for 15 minutes.

4. Bake mushroom caps until hot and bubbling, 10 to 15 minutes. Remove mushroom caps from oven and thinly slice diagonally. Cover loosely with foil and set aside.

5. Set oven to broil. Place bread on a foil-lined baking sheet and drizzle with olive oil and balsamic vinegar. Broil until golden and crisp. Top bread with arugula. Top each slice with three slices of tomato. Spread onions over top. Top with sliced mushrooms. Top each with three slices of mozzarella. Broil sandwiches until cheese is melted and bubbling.

6. Serve immediately.

Serves 4

Lime'n'Beer Marinated Skirt Steak Fajitas

For best results in getting a tender, well-flavoured skirt steak, marinate it for at least 24 hours. It will make your steak taste better.

2 bottles beer	Salt and black pepper
Juice of 3 limes	2 tbsp. chopped fresh cilantro
4 cloves garlic, minced	12 to 18 7-inch flour tortillas
2 lb. skirt steak	2 cups shredded iceberg lettuce
2 tbsp. Amazing Steak Spice (see page 43)	3 cups shredded pepper Jack cheese
2 tbsp. olive oil	1 cup Poker Salsa (see page 52)
1 large onion, sliced	1 cup Mango Guacamole (see page 54)
1 large green bell pepper, sliced	1 cup sour cream
1 large red bell pepper, sliced	

1. In a glass dish large enough to hold the skirt steak, whisk together the beer, lime juice and garlic. Using a sharp knife, score the skirt steaks on both sides in a diamond pattern, cutting 1 inch apart and 1/4 inch deep. Rub the steaks with the steak spice, pressing the spices into the meat. Add the steaks to the beer mixture, turning to coat. Marinate, covered and refrigerated, for at least 24 hours.

2. In a large frying pan over medium-high heat, heat the olive oil. Sauté the onion and green and red peppers for 4 to 6 minutes or until tender and lightly browned. Remove from heat. Season with salt and black pepper to taste and stir in cilantro. Set aside, keeping warm.

3. Heat a well-seasoned cast-iron grill pan over high heat in a well-ventilated kitchen. Remove steaks from marinade (discarding marinade) and pat steaks dry. Grill the steaks for 30 seconds to 1 minute per side for medium. Thinly slice steaks diagonally.

4. Warm tortillas in the microwave or oven. Spread shredded lettuce over tortillas. Top with a few slices of steak. Top with the onion mixture. Top with pepper Jack cheese.

5. Serve immediately, garnished with Poker Salsa, Mango Guacamole and sour cream.

Serves 6

Brick Oven Tacos

When I was growing up in Paris, Ontario, there were a lot of great things to do, but few restaurants to choose from. On the occasional late night after a good party, my friends and I had to go all the way to Brantford for tacos at The Brick Oven Pizza. Plain and simple, but a belly filler after a few pints.

1/2 lb. ground pork

1/2 lb. ground beef

3 tbsp. Mexican Chili Seasoning (see page 45)

3 tbsp. vegetable oil

1 medium onion, diced

4 cloves garlic, minced

2 jalapeño peppers, minced

1 medium red bell pepper, diced

Splash beer

1/4 cup Really Good Tomato Sauce (see page 73)

6 to 8 tsp. butter

6 to 8 corn tortillas (taco shells)

Dash hot sauce

2 cups shredded lettuce

1 cup Poker Salsa (see page 52)

1/2 cup sour cream

2 cups shredded Jack cheese

1. In a bowl, mix the pork, beef and Mexican Chili Seasoning. Marinate, covered and refrigerated, for 1 hour.

2. In a large frying pan, heat the oil over medium-high heat. Sauté the onion, garlic and jalapeño for 2 to 3 minutes or until tender. Add the seasoned meat and sauté, stirring to break up the meat, for 5 to 10 minutes, until the meat is cooked. Add the red pepper, beer and tomato sauce. Bring to a boil, reduce heat to low and simmer, stirring, for 10 to 15 minutes, until all the moisture has evaporated and the mixture is thick but still a little saucy. Set aside, keeping warm.

3. In another frying pan over medium-high heat, melt 1 tsp. of the butter. Fry a tortilla for 30 seconds to 1 minute per side, until a little crisp.

4. In your hand, fold the tortilla to form a U shape. Brush a dash of hot sauce along the bottom of the tortilla trough. Spoon in some of the meat mixture. Top with shredded lettuce, Poker Salsa, a dollop of sour cream and a load of cheese. Chomp and munch. Repeat with remaining tacos.

Serves 2 to 4

The Full Monty Cristo

This combination of the classic Western and a Monte Cristo is big—I mean really big. It'll thrill ya, it'll fill ya and it'll make ya wanna go back to bed. Great for rainy days and weekends.

1 ripe tomato, seeded and chopped

1 medium red bell pepper, thinly sliced

1/4 cup diced red onion

1 tbsp. chopped fresh parsley

Salt and black pepper

6 large eggs

3 tbsp. heavy cream

4 tbsp. butter

6 oz. shaved Black Forest ham

4 slices peameal bacon

4 thick slices white bread

1 cup shredded white Cheddar cheese

Splash Scotch

1. In a medium bowl, combine the tomato, red pepper, red onion and parsley. Season to taste with salt and black pepper. Mix well and set aside.
2. In a small bowl, lightly beat 2 of the eggs with 1 tbsp. of the cream. Season with salt and pepper.
3. In a medium nonstick frying pan over medium-low heat, melt 2 tbsp. of the butter. Scramble the eggs until just cooked through. Transfer eggs to a bowl and cover loosely with foil to keep warm.
4. In the same pan over medium-high heat, melt 1 tbsp. of the butter. Quickly fry the ham. Drain on paper towels. Set aside, keeping warm.
5. In the same pan over medium heat, fry the peameal bacon until cooked. Drain on paper towels. Set aside, keeping warm.
6. Preheat oven to 350°F. Line a baking sheet with foil.
7. Arrange two slices of bread on a cutting board and layer each with 1/4 cup of the cheese, the peameal bacon, scrambled eggs, tomato mixture, ham, the remaining cheese and a slice of bread. Firmly press to squish.
8. In a large bowl, whisk together the remaining 4 eggs, the remaining 2 tbsp. cream and a splash of Scotch.
9. In the same pan over medium-high heat, melt the remaining 1 tbsp. of butter. Dip a sandwich into the egg batter, letting the bread absorb some of the batter and get moist. Transfer immediately to the frying pan and fry 1 to 3 minutes per side or until golden brown. Transfer to the baking sheet. Repeat for the other sandwich. Using a spatula, press down firmly on the sandwich to squish.
10. Bake for 8 to 10 minutes, until all is heated and gooey. Cut each sandwich in half. Serve with defibrillator.

Serves 2

Root Beer Pulled Pork Sandwich

In the Great White North it is sometimes just too damn cold to spend 6 to 8 hours smoking a pork shoulder outside. This recipe brings it indoors. It requires a little patience, but the delicious results are well worth the wait.

You'll have leftover pork from this recipe. Freeze it for sandwiches, a topping for baked potatoes or a filling for quesadillas.

1 boneless pork shoulder (3 to 4 lb.)	1 1/4 cups + 1 tbsp. malt vinegar
1 small onion, sliced	2 1/2 cans root beer
4 cloves garlic, chopped	1 1/2 cups BBQ sauce
2 tbsp. Bone Dust BBQ Spice (see page 42)	Salt and pepper
1 tbsp. salt	4 dinner rolls
1 tsp. crushed red chilies	Colonel Mustard's Slaw (see page 109)

1. Place the pork shoulder in a stockpot. Add the onion, garlic, Bone Dust BBQ Spice, salt, chilies, 1 1/2 cups of the vinegar and 2 cans of the root beer. Add enough water to cover. Bring to a boil over high heat. Reduce heat to medium-low. Skim the scum from the surface. Simmer, uncovered, 2 to 2 1/2 hours, until pork easily tears when pulled with a fork.

2. Preheat oven to 400°F.

3. Transfer pork to a rack in a roasting pan. Roast for 30 minutes or until lightly browned on the outside. Let pork cool slightly until you can handle it with your hands. Using your hands, press the pork shoulder to break it apart. Using your fingers, shred or "pull" the pork into thin strands and clumps. Let cool.

4. Meanwhile, prepare the root beer sauce. In a small saucepan over medium-high heat, stir together the remaining 1/2 can of root beer, the BBQ sauce and the remaining 1 tbsp. of vinegar. Bring to a boil, reduce heat to low and keep warm.

5. Weigh out 1 1/2 lb. of pulled pork and place in a microwave-safe bowl. Add the root beer sauce and stir until the meat is coated with sauce. Cover bowl with plastic wrap, poke a hole in the plastic and microwave at High for 4 to 5 minutes, stirring occasionally, until heated through.

6. Serve on toasted buttered rolls topped with Colonel Mustard's Slaw.

Serves 4

Freddy's Cheese Steak Tenderloin Sandwich with Spicy Italian Hot Peppers

My friend Freddy made a version of this sandwich when he worked for me at the Skydome Hotel in Toronto, Ontario. This is worthy of a best sandwich award.

1/2 cup balsamic vinegar

2 tbsp. butter

Salt and pepper

4 beef tenderloin steaks (each 6 oz.)

1 to 2 tbsp. Amazing Steak Spice (see page 43)

1/2 cup + 3 tbsp. olive oil

1 small onion, cut into 1/2-inch slices

2 cloves garlic, minced

2 long red finger chilies, thinly sliced diagonally

4 long green Italian-style chilies, sliced diagonally

3 tbsp. white wine vinegar

1 tsp. sugar

1/2 tsp. salt

4 crusty rolls, halved

2 tbsp. Dijon mustard

12 leaves arugula

1/4 cup Really Good Tomato Sauce (see page 73), warmed

4 slices provolone cheese

4 slices prosciutto

1. In a small saucepan, bring balsamic vinegar to a boil over high heat. Reduce heat to medium and simmer for 10 to 12 minutes or until the vinegar has reduced by half. Remove from heat. Stir in the butter and season to taste with salt and pepper. Keep warm.
2. Cut steaks in half to make eight 2- to 3-oz. medallions. Rub steaks with the Steak Spice, pressing the spice into the meat. Set aside.

3. In a small frying pan, heat 1/4 cup of the olive oil over medium heat. Add onion, garlic and chilies. Sauté for 2 to 3 minutes or until tender. Stir in white wine vinegar, sugar and salt. Bring to a boil, stirring occasionally. Remove from heat and let cool.

4. In a medium frying pan over medium-high heat, heat 3 tbsp. of the olive oil. Fry the steak medallions, in batches, for 2 to 3 minutes per side for medium, basting with balsamic vinegar reduction. Remove from pan and keep warm.

5. Preheat the broiler. Line a baking sheet with foil.

6. Brush the cut side of the rolls with the remaining 1/4 cup of olive oil. Lightly toast the cut side of the rolls in the frying pan until golden and lightly crisp. Brush bottoms of buns with mustard and arrange on the baking sheet. Layer buns with arugula, steak medallions, the pepper mixture, a tablespoon of warmed Really Good Tomato Sauce, the provolone and the prosciutto. Broil the sandwiches until they are browned and the cheese is melting. Top with top half of buns. Serve immediately.

Serves 4

Seasonings, spicy rubs and a tempting paste

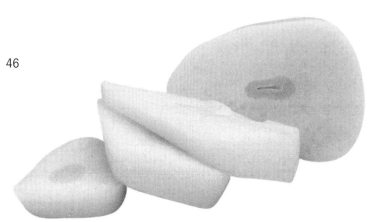

Bone Dust BBQ Spice

I first published this recipe in my *Sticks and Stones* cookbook, in 1999. It also appeared in my next three books and in 2002 was launched under my retail label, King of the Q. I get letters from fans who write: "This BBQ spice rules!"

1/2 cup paprika
1/4 cup chili powder
3 tbsp. salt
2 tbsp. sugar
2 tbsp. ground coriander
2 tbsp. garlic powder
2 tbsp. curry powder
2 tbsp. hot dry mustard
1 tbsp. black pepper
1 tbsp. dried basil
1 tbsp. dried thyme
1 tbsp. ground cumin
1 tbsp. cayenne pepper

Mix all the ingredients together. Store in a tightly sealed container away from heat and light.

Makes about 2 1/2 cups

Amazing Steak Spice

Also known as Montreal Steak Spice, this has got to be the best rub for steaks. It truly is my favourite. I believe that the saltier the rub, the better the steak will be. (Look for my Amazing Steak Spice at a retailer near you.)

1/2 cup coarse kosher salt
1/4 cup coarsely ground black pepper
1/4 cup coarsely ground white pepper
1/4 cup mustard seeds
1/4 cup cracked coriander seeds
1/4 cup granulated garlic
1/4 cup granulated onion
1/4 cup crushed red chilies
1/4 cup dill seeds

Mix all the ingredients together. Store in a tightly sealed container away from heat and light.

Makes 2 1/2 cups

Bayou Bite Cajun Rub

Legend has it that this Cajun seasoning, when put on the tip of an alligator's nose, will cause the gator to sneeze. Maybe we can get the guys from the movie *Jackass* to test that out for us.

2 tbsp. salt

2 tbsp. paprika

2 tbsp. cayenne pepper

1 tbsp. sugar

1 tbsp. hot mustard powder

1 tbsp. black pepper

1 tbsp. white pepper

1 tbsp. garlic powder

1 tbsp. onion powder

2 tsp. ground cumin

1 tsp. dried oregano

1 tsp. dried thyme

1 tsp. dried sage

1 tsp. ground coriander

Mix all the ingredients together. Store in a tightly sealed container away from heat and light.

Makes about 1 cup

Mexican Chili Seasoning

Arriba! It's spicy good! Great for chilies, stews, grill-rubbing and meatballs.

1/4 cup salt

3 tbsp. ancho or Mexican chili powder

3 tbsp. paprika

2 tbsp. ground cumin

2 tbsp. cayenne pepper

1 tbsp. black pepper

2 tsp. garlic powder

2 tsp. onion powder

1 tsp. dried oregano

1 tsp. dried thyme

1 tsp. hot dry mustard

Mix all the ingredients together. Store in a tightly sealed container away from heat and light.

Makes about 1 1/2 cups

Cochin Curry Masala Seasoning

There I was, hot on the spice trail in India, trying to sidestep freakin' bugs the size of Volkswagens everywhere. And the cobras, too. In fact, I spent most of my time swatting and running (okay, just swatting—I don't run). However, I did stumble across this tasty Cochin curry seasoning.

1/4 cup ground cumin

3 tbsp. turmeric

1 tbsp. salt

1 tbsp. ground ginger

1 tbsp. ground coriander

1 tbsp. black pepper

1 tbsp. dry mustard

2 tsp. cinnamon

2 tsp. crushed red chilies

1 tsp. ground fennel

1 tsp. grated nutmeg

1 tsp. ground mace

Mix all the ingredients together. Store in a tightly sealed container away from heat and light. Will keep for up to 3 months.

Makes about 3/4 cup

Garlic Herb Steak Paste

Rub this one all over your favourite steak. It's soooo good.

2 heads garlic, peeled and minced

1/4 cup Amazing Steak Spice (see page 43)

1/4 cup chopped fresh herbs (such as parsley, sage, rosemary and thyme)

1/4 cup olive oil

Mix all the ingredients together. Store in a tightly sealed container, refrigerated, for up to 1 week.

Makes about 1 1/4 cups

Appetizing dips,
bites and starters

Clam Dip

While watching the ball game, have lots of chips on hand to dunk into this awesome clam dip. It's a beautiful thing. You can use 1 cup of drained canned clams if you wish; just skip the steaming step.

2 lb. steamer clams, rinsed well

1/2 cup beer

1 cup cream cheese, softened

1/2 cup mayonnaise

1/2 cup sour cream

1 green onion, chopped

1 small shallot, chopped

1 tsp. Bone Dust BBQ Spice (see page 42)

1 tsp. lemon juice

Dash hot sauce

Salt and pepper

1. Combine the clams and the beer in a large pot. Cover, bring to a boil and steam the clams for 6 to 8 minutes or until the clams open. Remove from heat. Discard any unopened clams and let clams cool. Remove clam meat from shells. Discard shells.

2. In a food processor, cream together the cream cheese, mayonnaise and sour cream. Add the clams, green onion, shallot, Bone Dust BBQ Spice, lemon juice and hot sauce. Pulse until fully mixed but still a little coarse. Season to taste with salt and pepper.

3. Transfer to a serving dish. Dunk your chips, pretzels, tortillas or vegetables. Cheers! (No double dipping, please.)

Serves 4 to 8

Crab and Artichoke Gooey Dip

This appetizer is a party favourite. Have lots of bread and chips on hand for dipping.

1 cup Really Good Béchamel Sauce (see page 74)

1 cup fresh lump crab meat

1 can (14 oz./398 g) artichoke hearts, drained and cut in quarters

1/2 cup shredded Swiss cheese

1/2 cup shredded mozzarella cheese

1 green onion, finely chopped

2 tbsp. white wine

1 tbsp. chopped fresh herbs (such as parsley, basil and thyme)

Salt and pepper

Pinch Bone Dust BBQ Spice (see page 42)

1/4 cup grated Parmesan cheese

1. In a bowl, combine the béchamel, crab meat, artichoke hearts, Swiss cheese, mozzarella cheese, green onion, wine and herbs. Season to taste with salt and pepper and a pinch or two of Bone Dust BBQ Spice. Mix thoroughly.
2. Butter a 4- to 6-cup casserole dish. Pour in crab mixture. Sprinkle evenly with Parmesan cheese. Cover and refrigerate for at least 1 hour to set.
3. Preheat oven to 425°F. Bake dip, uncovered, until hot and bubbling, 20 to 30 minutes.
4. Serve immediately with fresh bread or chips for dipping and drooling.

Serves 4

Poker Salsa

Made this for my poker buddies Cal, Chris and Ed while on a golfing trip in Hilton Head, South Carolina. I won large. Musta been the salsa.

1/2 pint grape tomatoes, quartered
1 small onion, diced
1 cubanelle pepper, diced
1 red bell pepper, diced
1 jalapeño pepper, finely chopped
3 tomatillos, chopped
2 green onions, finely chopped
4 cloves garlic, minced
3 tbsp. olive oil
Juice of 1 lime
Few dashes chipotle Tabasco sauce
Splash beer
Salt, pepper and Bone Dust BBQ Spice (see page 42)

1. In a medium bowl, combine tomatoes, onion, cubanelle pepper, red pepper, jalapeño pepper, tomatillos, green onions, garlic, olive oil, lime juice, hot sauce and beer. Season to taste with salt, pepper and Bone Dust BBQ Spice. Let stand for 1 hour.
2. Serve with tortilla chips, fajitas or nachos.

Serves 4

Beet Stack with Green Apples and Ermite Blue Cheese with Vanilla Champagne Vinaigrette (page 98)

Oven-Baked Carb-Free Frittata (page 6)

Smoky Bacon Blue Cheese Dip

I first tasted something like this dip at New York's Blue Smoke BBQ Restaurant. Here's my version. It's thick and rich and loaded with bacon, so you had better make lots—it's sure to go fast!

3 slices thick-cut double-smoked bacon

1 1/2 cups sour cream

1/2 cup mayonnaise

1/2 cup cream cheese

1 to 2 tbsp. lemon juice

1 tsp. Bone Dust BBQ Spice (see page 42)

1 green onion, chopped

1 tbsp. chopped fresh thyme

Dash hot sauce

Splash Worcestershire sauce

1 cup crumbled Roquefort cheese

Salt and pepper

1. Cut the bacon into 1/4-inch dice. In a frying pan over medium-high heat, fry the bacon until crisp. Drain bacon on paper towels and let cool.
2. In a food processor, combine the sour cream, mayonnaise, cream cheese, lemon juice and Bone Dust BBQ Spice. Blend until smooth. Add green onion, thyme, hot sauce and Worcestershire sauce; pulse until mixed. Transfer to a bowl and stir in bacon and Roquefort cheese. Season to taste with salt and pepper. Cover and refrigerate for at least 1 hour.
3. Serve with chips, nachos, tortilla chips, vegetable sticks and pretzels.

Makes about 3 1/2 cups

Mango Guacamole

I love guacamole. It's a great appetizer for any party. This one is made with sweet, ripe mango. It's sure to get your mojo going.

2 ripe avocados

Juice of 1 lime

2 green onions, chopped

1 long hot red chili, seeded and minced

1/2 cup diced ripe mango

1/4 cup diced sweet onion (such as Vidalia)

2 tbsp. chopped fresh cilantro

2 tbsp. olive oil

1 tsp. minced fresh ginger

Salt and pepper

1. In a medium bowl, mash the avocados with a fork. Stir in lime juice. Stir in green onions, chili, mango, sweet onion, cilantro, oil and ginger. Season to taste with salt and pepper.
2. Guacamole keeps for up to 3 days refrigerated.

Makes 2 to 3 cups

Cedar-Planked Brie with Grilled Pineapple Topping

By far this is the best party appetizer—a must-have recipe for any occasion.

3 1/2-inch-thick slices ripe pineapple

2 tbsp. vegetable oil

1 jalapeño pepper, finely chopped

3 shallots, thinly sliced

1/2 cup pineapple marmalade or orange marmalade

1/4 cup white wine

2 green onions, thinly sliced

1 tbsp. chopped fresh thyme

Salt and pepper

2 Brie wheels (each 250 g)

Special equipment: 1 untreated cedar plank
    (at least 6 x 12 inches and 1/2 inch thick),
    soaked in cold water for at least 1 hour

1. Preheat grill to high.
2. Grill the pineapple slices for 2 to 3 minutes per side or until lightly charred. Set aside to cool. Coarsely chop the pineapple and set aside.
3. In a medium saucepan over medium-high heat, heat the vegetable oil. Sauté the jalapeño and shallots for 1 to 2 minutes, until tender. Add wine and marmalade, stirring until the marmalade becomes liquid. Remove from heat and stir in the grilled pineapple, green onions and thyme. Season to taste with salt and pepper. Let cool completely.
4. Evenly space the Brie wheels on the plank. Top each piece of Brie with the pineapple mixture, being sure to load it on. Place planked Brie on the grill and close lid. Bake for 5 minutes. Carefully open the lid; if the plank is on fire, spray it with water and reduce heat to medium. Close lid and continue to bake Brie for 8 to 10 minutes, until the Brie is golden brown, soft and beginning to bulge. Be careful not to let the cheese burst—the insides will ooze out and you will lose all the precious and decadent ooey, gooey cheese.
5. Serve immediately on the plank with lots of bread and crackers.

Serves 8 to 12

Tip: To prepare this dish in the oven, preheat oven to 450°F. Place the plank (you don't have to soak it this time) in a 2-inch-deep baking pan. Pour water around the plank until it floats. Preheat plank in oven for 10 minutes or until you can smell the cedar. Place Brie on plank and bake for 15 minutes or until cheese bulges and is warmed through and the rind takes on a smoky tinge. Add more water to the pan if necessary.

Coulson's Spicy Pickled Eggs

This recipe is from my friend David Coulson of Napoleon BBQ Co. I first tasted these beauties at David's Freeze Your Ringers Off Horseshoe Tournament, which takes place in the freezing cold of February.

Get four good friends together and watch football. Eat eggs, three each. Eat chili (see page 138). Drink beer (it's in the fridge, duh). Fun, eh?

2 habanero or Scotch bonnet peppers

12 large eggs

1 tbsp. vegetable oil

1 small red onion, sliced

4 cloves garlic, chopped

1/4 cup kosher salt

1 tbsp. coarsely ground white pepper

1 tbsp. Bone Dust BBQ Spice (see page 42)

6 cups white vinegar

Special equipment: a 1-quart preserving jar

1. Cut open the peppers and cut out the white membrane and seeds. Finely chop the membrane and seeds. Coarsely chop the peppers. Set aside.
2. In a large saucepan, cover eggs with cold water. Bring to a boil. Cover, remove from heat and let stand for 14 minutes. Drain and run under cold running water to cool slightly.
3. Peel eggs while they are still warm (the shells will come away a little easier). Puncture each egg with a fork three times to allow the pickling liquid to get into the egg more easily. Put eggs in the preserving jar.
4. In a well-ventilated kitchen, in a medium frying pan over medium-high heat, heat the oil. Sauté the habanero peppers (with the membranes and seeds), red onion and garlic until tender, 1 to 2 minutes. The peppers are spicy, so watch out for the fumes. Stir in the kosher salt, white pepper and Bone Dust BBQ Spice. Spoon mixture into the jar.
5. In a saucepan bring the vinegar to a boil. Pour the vinegar into the preserving jar. Seal the jar and turn it upside down a few times to disperse the ingredients. Cool to lukewarm, then refrigerate.
6. Let eggs pickle for at least 2 weeks, turning the jar upside down once each day.
7. Although these eggs are best soon after they are pickled, they will keep up to 3 months refrigerated.

Makes 12 eggs

Caution: Only open this jar outside, unless your significant other has absolutely no sense of smell.

Tender Fried Calamari with Red Pepper Rouille

The key to good fried calamari is to marinate it first in buttermilk. The buttermilk gives the squid a tender texture so that it's not rubbery and tough.

1 lb. fresh or thawed frozen whole squid (approximately 8 bodies)

2 cups buttermilk

1 cup all-purpose flour

1 cup corn flour (not cornmeal)

1 tbsp. Bone Dust BBQ Spice (see page 42)

6 cups vegetable oil, for frying

Red Pepper Rouille

1 medium roasted red bell pepper

1 roasted red jalapeño pepper

1 clove garlic, chopped

1 cup mayonnaise

1/2 cup cream cheese

1 tsp. lemon juice

Dash hot sauce

Salt and black pepper to taste

1 tbsp. chopped fresh cilantro

1. To clean the squid, pull the head and tentacles away from the body; set aside. Remove and discard the hard beak from the head. Hold the tail firmly and pull on the hard, transparent backbone to remove the bone and the innards. With a knife, carefully scrape away any remaining innards. Peel away the outer membrane and discard. You should be left with a clean, hollow tube.

2. Rinse the body under cold water and pat dry inside and out. Cut the body crosswise three-quarters of the way through the flesh, every 1/2 inch. It should look like a fan, slashed down one side but still connected on the other. Soak the tentacles and body in the buttermilk, covered and refrigerated, for 3 to 4 hours.

3. Meanwhile, make the Red Pepper Rouille. Peel and seed the bell pepper. Coarsely chop the bell pepper and jalapeño pepper. In a food processor, combine the peppers, garlic, mayonnaise, cream cheese, lemon juice, hot sauce, salt and black pepper. Blend until smooth. Stir in cilantro. Set aside.

4. In a medium bowl, combine the all-purpose flour, corn flour and Bone Dust BBQ Spice.

5. Drain the squid well and pat dry with paper towels. Toss the squid in the flour mixture to evenly coat, shaking off excess flour.

6. Heat the oil in a large, heavy pot to 375°F. Deep-fry the squid in batches (returning oil to 375°F between batches), until golden brown and crispy. Drain squid on paper towels.

7. Serve immediately with Red Pepper Rouille.

Serves 4

Smokin' Beer BBQ Steamed Mussels

I devised this recipe for a "King of the Q" menu at Shoeless Joe's Restaurants in the Toronto area. Caution: these are addictive! Allow a pound of mussels per person.

2 lb. fresh mussels

2 tbsp. Bone Dust BBQ Spice (see page 42)

2 tbsp. olive oil

4 cloves garlic, minced

1 large jalapeño pepper, finely chopped

1/2 cup diced onion

1/3 bottle dark lager

3 tbsp. butter

1/3 cup gourmet BBQ sauce

Salt and pepper

2 green onions, thinly sliced

1. Scrub and beard the mussels and drain them in a colander. Toss mussels in Bone Dust BBQ Spice to evenly coat.
2. In a large pot over high heat, heat the oil. Add the garlic, jalapeño and onion; sauté for 1 to 2 minutes or until the garlic is fragrant. Add the mussels and stir for 1 minute. Add the beer and cover.
3. Steam mussels for 5 to 8 minutes, occasionally shaking the pot. The mussels are done when the shells have opened. Remove from heat and discard any unopened mussels.
4. Add the butter and BBQ sauce, stirring until the butter is melted and the mussels are evenly coated in the sauce. Season to taste with salt and pepper.
5. Spoon mussels into two large serving bowls and garnish with the green onions. Serve with fresh crusty bread for sauce-dunking and mussel-slurping.

Serves 2

Bahamian Grouper Fingers with Lime Aïoli

Grouper is the fish of the Bahamas. Tender, white flesh with a rich buttery texture make this snack a big hit.

Lime Aïoli

1 anchovy fillet, mashed

1/4 cup mashed potato

2 egg yolks

1 tsp. Dijon mustard

1/2 tsp. ground white pepper

Juice of 2 limes

3/4 cup olive oil

Salt

2 lb. boneless skinless grouper fillet

Juice of 1 lime

2 tbsp. Bone Dust BBQ Spice (see page 42)

1 cup vegetable oil

1 cup all-purpose flour

2 eggs

1. Prepare the Lime Aïoli. In a food processor, blend the anchovy, mashed potato, egg yolks, mustard, pepper and lime juice. With the motor running, add oil in a steady stream and blend until smooth. Season to taste with salt. Set aside.
2. Cut the grouper into finger-size pieces. In a bowl, gently toss the grouper with the lime juice and 1 tbsp. of the Bone Dust BBQ Spice.
3. Combine the flour and remaining 1 tbsp. of Bone Dust in a shallow bowl. In another shallow bowl, beat the eggs. Dip each grouper finger in the egg, letting the excess drip off, and then dredge in the flour.
4. In a large frying pan over medium-high heat, heat the oil. Fry the grouper fingers in batches, without crowding the pan, for 2 to 3 minutes per side, until golden brown and cooked through. Drain on paper towels.
5. Serve with the Lime Aïoli.

Serves 6

Drunken Tuna Tartare Spoon Hors d'Oeuvres

This is one of those fancy shmancy hors d'oeuvres that not only looks great when served but tastes absolutely outstanding!

1/2 lb. fresh sushi-grade tuna

1/4 cup soy sauce

1/4 cup sake, plus addition for drizzling

2 tbsp. mirin

1 tbsp. olive oil

2 tsp. pickled ginger, finely chopped

1 tsp. sugar

1/2 tsp. toasted sesame seeds

1/2 tsp. wasabi paste

Splash fish sauce

Squeeze lime juice

1 green onion, finely chopped

1 tbsp. finely chopped shallot

1 tbsp. chopped fresh cilantro

Salt and pepper

1. Place tuna in freezer for 15 minutes to firm it up before slicing.
2. Meanwhile, in a medium bowl, combine soy sauce, sake, mirin, oil, pickled ginger, sugar, sesame seeds, wasabi paste, fish sauce and lime juice. Whisk until wasabi is dissolved.
3. Using a sharp knife, trim the tuna of any dark flesh. Cut the tuna into 1/4-inch cubes. Add to soy sauce mixture. Add green onion, shallot, cilantro and salt and pepper to taste. Mix gently. Refrigerate for 15 minutes to chill.
4. Spoon small dollops of tuna tartare onto tablespoons. (I like to use Chinese soupspoons because they have a deep bowl.) Drizzle tuna with sake and serve.

Serves 12

Oven-Planked Peppered Trout Bruschetta

I first made this appetizer after a fishing trip in Algonquin Park with my buds. We hooked a mess of trout and after returning home with our bounty (the legal limit, mind you), I decided a good planking was in order.

4 cups liquid (beer, apple juice, water or a combination)

4 trout fillets (each 6 oz.), skin on

Salt and pepper

1/4 cup diced shallots

1/4 cup chopped chives

3 tbsp. finely grated fresh horseradish

1 tbsp. minced capers

1 tbsp. white wine vinegar

2 tbsp. cracked black pepper

Sea salt to taste

Dash hot sauce

1/2 cup olive oil

16 slices baguette

Dill sprigs, for garnish

Special equipment: 1 untreated cedar plank (at least 6 x 12 inches and 1/2 inch thick), soaked in cold water for at least 1 hour

1. Preheat oven to 425°F.
2. Set the plank in a 2-inch-deep roasting pan large enough to hold it and add the 4 cups of liquid; the plank should float (add more liquid if necessary). Place in the oven for 5 to 8 minutes. When you can smell the cedar, season the trout with salt and pepper to taste. Evenly space the trout, skin side down, on the plank and bake for 15 to 20 minutes, until the fish is cooked through, flaky and has a smoky colour. Carefully remove plank from liquid and allow trout to cool. (The trout can be made up to this point and refrigerated for up to 3 days.)
3. Remove skin and flake the trout. In a bowl, combine the trout, shallots, chives, horseradish, capers, vinegar, black pepper, sea salt and hot sauce. Set aside.
4. In a large frying pan, heat the olive oil over medium-high heat. Fry the baguette slices, in batches, for 2 minutes per side or until lightly browned and crisp. Drain on paper towels and let cool.
5. Top each slice of toast with 1 to 2 tbsp. of the smoked trout mixture. Garnish with a sprig of dill.

Serves 4 to 8

Grilled Texas Shrimp Wrapped in Beef Tenderloin

While on a behind-the-scenes tour of the Houston Space Center, I had an opportunity to fly the space shuttle simulator. We also sampled some "space food." Needs work, baby, needs work. Now this is the kind of food astronauts should have in space.

BBQ Sauce

1/4 cup corn syrup

1/4 cup ketchup

1 oz. Jack Daniel's

1 tbsp. chopped fresh cilantro

1 chipotle pepper, minced

Bone Dust BBQ Spice (see page 42)

Salt and pepper

2 lb. beef tenderloin

16 jumbo shrimp (12–15/lb. count), peeled and deveined

6 oz. Jack Daniel's

2 to 3 tbsp. Bone Dust BBQ Spice (see page 42)

2 to 3 tbsp. oil

Special equipment: a Cajun injector

1. Freeze the beef for 15 minutes to make it easier to slice.
2. Meanwhile, prepare the BBQ sauce. In a bowl, whisk together the corn syrup, ketchup, Jack Daniel's, cilantro and chipotle pepper. Season to taste with a good pinch of Bone Dust BBQ Spice and salt and pepper. Set aside.
3. Preheat grill to medium-high.
4. Thinly slice beef into 1- to 2-oz. slices. Using your fingers, gently flatten each slice.
5. Using a Cajun injector or syringe, inject each shrimp with Jack Daniel's. Season shrimp with some of the Bone Dust BBQ Spice. Wrap each shrimp with 1 to 2 slices of the beef, pressing firmly around the middle so the beef adheres. Brush with oil and season with more Bone Dust. Skewer the shrimp onto chopsticks or soaked bamboo or metal skewers.
6. Grill for 2 to 3 minutes per side, until the shrimp are just cooked and the beef is lightly charred. Baste with reserved BBQ sauce and serve immediately.

Serves 6 to 8

Note: A Cajun injector is a large syringe used for injecting marinades into meats. Look for these injectors in kitchen and BBQ supply stores, or at www.napoleongrills.com.

Garlicky Escargot-Stuffed Mushroom Caps

I remember the first time I had escargots. It was on a ski trip to Vermont with my brother Edward. I was 16, and it was a big deal going away with my older brother. The escargots were garlicky and loaded with butter, the beer crisp and cold, and the powder snow deep. What a trip!

12 large white mushroom caps

3 tbsp. balsamic vinegar

3 tbsp. olive oil

Salt and pepper

4 tbsp. butter

6 to 8 cloves garlic, minced

1/2 cup diced sweet onion

24 to 36 canned escargots, rinsed and drained

3 tbsp. chopped fresh herbs (such as parsley and thyme)

2 tbsp. dry sherry

1/4 cup grated Romano cheese

1/4 cup dry bread crumbs

1. Preheat oven to 375°F. Line a baking sheet with foil.
2. Run your finger around the inside of each mushroom cap to create more of a well.
3. In a medium bowl, combine mushrooms caps, balsamic vinegar and oil. Season to taste with salt and pepper and gently mix to evenly coat. Place mushrooms, gill side up, on the baking sheet. Bake for 12 to 15 minutes or until the mushroom caps are lightly browned and tender. Drain caps, gill side down, on paper towels. Set aside the baking sheet; do not turn off the oven.
4. In a medium frying pan, melt the butter over medium-high heat. Add the garlic and onion; sauté until tender, 2 to 3 minutes. Add escargots and sauté until escargots are heated through, 2 to 3 minutes. Remove from heat and stir in herbs and sherry. Season to taste with salt and pepper. Let cool slightly.
5. Pat mushroom caps dry with paper towels and arrange on the baking sheet. Spoon 2 or 3 escargots into each mushroom cap. Top with remaining garlic mixture.
6. Combine Romano cheese and bread crumbs. Top each mushroom cap with about 2 tsp. of the cheese mixture. Bake for 10 to 12 minutes, until mushrooms are heated through and the cheese is golden brown and crispy. Serve immediately.

Serves 4 to 6

Bacon-Wrapped Crab Claws

This is my favourite seafood hors d'oeuvre. It's a bit of work to prepare, and patience is everything, but it's well worth the effort. It is also great grilled over medium-low heat until the bacon is crispy and the claws are heated through

3/4 lb. flounder, drained and gently squeezed of any excess water
1 cup crab meat, drained and squeezed of any excess water
2 egg whites
1/3 cup heavy cream
1 tbsp. lemon juice
1 tbsp. Bone Dust BBQ Spice (see page 42)
16 to 20 snow crab claws, half cracked
16 to 20 slices bacon
Your favourite cocktail sauce

1. In a food processor, blend the flounder, crab, egg whites, cream, lemon juice and Bone Dust BBQ Spice until smooth. Divide mixture into 16 to 20 portions (depending on the number of crab claws you have) and shape each portion into a ball.
2. Insert the meat side of a crab claw into each ball, using your hands to make a smooth, tight ball around the base of the claw. Place on a lightly greased tray and freeze until firm, 1 to 2 hours.
3. Wrap the base of each frozen claw with 1 slice of bacon, stretching the bacon so it sticks to itself and seals onto the crab ball. Freeze claws for 1 hour. (Claws can be prepared to this point and frozen for up to 6 months.)
4. Preheat oven to 400°F.
5. Place the frozen crab claws on a nonstick baking sheet. Bake for 30 to 40 minutes, turning occasionally to ensure even browning, until the crab is hot and the bacon is crisp.
6. Serve hot with cocktail sauce for dipping.

Serves 8 to 10

Roasted Marrow Bones

Marrow is extremely rich—a little goes a long way. Ask your butcher for large marrow bones, which have more marrow for slurping. This recipe is pure decadence. Be sure to serve this with a great Merlot.

3 to 4 lb. fresh marrow bones
Coarse sea salt
Coarsely ground black pepper
1 baguette
Dash well-aged balsamic vinegar

1. Preheat oven to 425°F.
2. Sprinkle cut side of the marrow bones with salt and pepper. Place marrow bones, cut side down, in a roasting pan. Roast for 30 to 40 minutes, until bones are lightly browned and the marrow is bubbling.
3. Towards the end of the cooking time, wrap the baguette in foil. Bake until heated through, about 10 minutes. Remove from foil and slice.
4. Using a small spoon, remove the marrow from the bones and spread on the warm bread. Season with salt and pepper to taste and a dash of balsamic vinegar. Serve immediately.

Serves 4

Beer Nut–Crusted Crunchy Chicken Tenders with Chili-Infused Honey

Mmmm, beer nuts. Crunchy sweet, they make an unusual breading for chicken. This is bar food at its tastiest.

1 1/2 lb. chicken tenderloins, trimmed of sinew
1 bottle beer
1 tbsp. Bone Dust BBQ Spice (see page 42)
1 cup all-purpose flour
3 large eggs
1/4 cup cream
1 1/2 cups panko (Japanese bread crumbs)
1 cup coarsely ground beer nuts

1. In a large bowl, stir together chicken, beer and Bone Dust BBQ Spice. Marinate, covered and refrigerated, for 2 to 4 hours. Drain.
2. Preheat oven to 425°F. Line a baking sheet with foil.
3. Place flour in a bowl. In a second bowl, whisk together eggs and cream. In a third bowl, combine panko and beer nuts. Dredge chicken in flour. Dip into egg mixture, letting excess run off, and then dredge in the panko breading, pressing gently to make the breading adhere. Arrange chicken on the baking sheet. Bake, turning once, for 15 to 20 minutes, until cooked through and golden brown.
4. Serve with Chili-Infused Honey, for dipping.

Serves 6 to 8

Chili-Infused Honey

1 cup honey
1 to 2 sprigs thyme
1 to 2 fresh hot red chilies, finely chopped

In a small saucepan over medium heat, bring the honey, thyme and chilies to a low boil. Remove from heat and let stand for 4 to 6 hours. Discard thyme.

Makes about 1 cup

Maple BBQ Oven-Roasted Wings

Wet naps, finger bowls, napkins and warmed kitchen towels are what you'll need to clean up after this sticky wing fest!

3 lb. jumbo chicken wings (8 to 10 pieces/lb.)

2 tbsp. Bone Dust BBQ Spice (see page 42)

2 tbsp. vegetable oil

1/2 cup BBQ sauce

1/4 cup brown sugar

1/4 cup maple syrup

2 tbsp. melted butter

1 tbsp. lemon juice

1. Remove wing tips and cut the wings in half at the joint. In a large bowl, combine the wing pieces, Bone Dust BBQ Spice and oil. Mix to evenly coat. Marinate, covered and refrigerated, for 1 hour.
2. Preheat oven to 425°F. Line a baking sheet with foil.
3. In a large bowl, whisk together the BBQ sauce, sugar, maple syrup, butter and lemon juice. Set sauce aside.
4. Arrange the wings in a single layer on the baking sheet. Bake for 40 to 45 minutes, turning once, until wings are just cooked and evenly browned. Transfer wings to the sauce and toss to coat. Return wings to the baking sheet and bake another 10 minutes or until sticky and crisp.
5. Serve immediately with Smoky Bacon Blue Cheese Dip (see page 53).

Serves 4 to 6

Stocks, sauces and soups

Really Good Beef (or Veal) Stock

To make beef or veal stock into demi-glace, a thickened stock that is used in sauces, bring the strained stock to a rolling boil. Reduce heat to medium and simmer until the stock has reduced by half. Use in sauces for beef, game, veal, lamb and mushrooms.

10 lb. beef or veal bones, including knuckles

4 stalks celery, cut into 2-inch pieces

3 large carrots, cut into 1-inch pieces

2 large onions, quartered

1 large leek, cut into 1-inch pieces

1/2 bunch fresh thyme

1/2 bunch flat-leaf parsley

2 bay leaves

1 tbsp. peppercorns

1 tbsp. salt

1. Preheat oven to 400°F.
2. Spread the bones in a large roasting pan and roast for 1 hour, turning regularly to get an even, dark golden-brown colour. Add the celery, carrots, onions and leek; roast for 30 minutes. Let cool slightly.
3. Transfer the bones and vegetables to a large stockpot. Add the thyme, parsley, bay leaves, peppercorns and salt. Cover with cold water. Bring to a rolling boil over high heat. Do not stir. Skim the grey foam from the surface. Reduce heat to medium-low and simmer, without stirring, for 4 hours or until the stock is full-flavoured.
4. Let stock cool slightly. Strain the stock; do not press on the solids. Let cool completely. Stock keeps refrigerated for up to 7 days or frozen for 3 months.

Makes about 16 cups

Really Good Roasted Chicken Stock

I like roasting my chicken bones before making chicken stock. It intensifies the stock, resulting in a richer flavour. Use in soups, sauces, casseroles and any dish that requires chicken stock.

2 lb. chicken wings

8 cloves garlic, smashed

1 large onion, chopped

2 medium carrots, chopped

2 stalks celery, chopped

8 peppercorns

2 sprigs fresh thyme

2 sprigs fresh parsley

2 sprigs fresh sage or rosemary

2 bay leaves

1. Preheat oven to 375°F.
2. Spread the chicken wings in a large roasting pan and roast, turning and shaking the pan to keep the wings from sticking, for 45 minutes to 1 hour, until golden brown.
3. Transfer wings to a large stockpot. Add the garlic, onion, carrots, celery, peppercorns, thyme, parsley, sage and bay leaves. Cover with cold water. Bring to a rolling boil, uncovered. Do not stir. Skim any grey scum from the surface. Reduce heat to medium-low and simmer, without stirring, for 2 hours, skimming the scum as required.
4. Strain the stock. Let cool completely. Stock keeps refrigerated for up to 7 days or frozen for 3 months.

Makes 12 to 16 cups

Really Good Fish Stock

Use fish bones from white-fleshed saltwater fish such as grouper, halibut, snapper and cod. Avoid salmon bones, which tend to give the stock too strong a flavour.

3 lb. fish bones and heads
1 small leek, washed and chopped
1 large onion, chopped
2 stalks celery, chopped
1 large carrot, chopped
1 sprig fresh thyme
1 sprig fresh dill
2 bay leaves
6 peppercorns
1 tsp. sea salt
1/2 tsp. dill seeds

1. Place the fish bones and heads, leek, onion, celery, carrot, thyme, dill, bay leaves, peppercorns, salt and dill seeds in a large stockpot. Cover with cold water. Bring to a rolling boil over high heat. Do not stir. Skim the scum from the surface. Reduce heat to medium-low and simmer, without stirring, for 30 minutes, skimming as required.
2. Strain through a sieve lined with four layers of cheesecloth. Let cool completely. Stock keeps refrigerated for up to 7 days or frozen for 3 months.

Makes 12 to 16 cups

Really Good Tomato Sauce

For some reason every race car driver I cook for likes my tomato sauce. I consistently made 2 gallons of tomato sauce every CART race. Roberto Moreno likes his on capellini pasta. Adrian Fernandez likes his on grilled chicken. Darren Manning likes his spicy, and Alex Tagliani likes his on steamed rice. This is my recipe for quick and easy tomato sauce.

2 tbsp. olive oil

1 large onion, finely diced

6 cloves garlic, minced

1 large roasted red bell pepper, diced

3 cans (each 28 oz./796 mL) plum tomatoes, seeded and coarsely chopped, juices reserved

3 tbsp. chopped fresh basil

Splash balsamic vinegar

Salt and pepper

1. In a large pot over medium heat, heat the oil. Add the onions, garlic and red pepper; cook for 8 to 10 minutes or until the onions are translucent and soft. Add the tomatoes and their juice. Simmer, uncovered and stirring occasionally, for 30 minutes.
2. Stir in the basil and cook for a few more minutes. Season with balsamic vinegar, and salt and pepper to taste. Let cool completely. Tomato sauce keeps refrigerated for up to 5 days or frozen for 4 months.

Makes 8 cups

Really Good Béchamel Sauce

Béchamel is a basic "mother sauce," or base sauce, for many cream and cheese sauces. For the world's simplest cheese sauce, add 2 cups of your favourite shredded cheese.

1/4 cup butter

1/3 cup + 2 tbsp. all-purpose flour

6 cups milk

1 small onion, quartered

2 cloves garlic

1 bay leaf

1 tsp. dry mustard

1 tsp. salt

Pinch grated nutmeg

1/2 cup heavy cream

Salt and white pepper to taste

1. In a medium saucepan, melt the butter over medium heat. Stir in the flour until smooth. Cook, stirring, for 5 minutes. Add the milk, 1 cup at a time, stirring constantly to remove all lumps. Add the onion, garlic, bay leaf, mustard, salt and nutmeg. Stir in the cream. Slowly bring the sauce to a simmer, stirring constantly, until sauce is thick and smooth, about 20 minutes. Do not let boil.
2. Strain béchamel. Adjust seasoning with salt and pepper. Let cool completely if not using immediately in a recipe.

Makes about 4 cups

Super Cheesy Broccoli and Cheese Soup with Walnut-Crusted Cheese Balls

In the kitchen at Rogerson Lodges, I used to make a broccoli and cheese soup for the fishing guides and resort staff. It was thick and loaded with broccoli and cheese. This is my updated, even cheesier recipe.

1 large bunch broccoli (choose a real biggie)

1/4 cup butter

4 cloves garlic, minced

1 medium onion, diced

2 stalks celery, diced

1/4 cup dry sherry

1/4 cup + 2 tbsp. all-purpose flour

8 cups Really Good Roasted Chicken Stock (see page 71)

1/4 cup chopped fresh parsley

1 cup shredded sharp Cheddar cheese

1/2 cup softened cream cheese

1/4 cup grated Parmesan cheese

1/4 tsp. cayenne pepper

Dash Worcestershire sauce

Grated nutmeg to taste

Salt and black pepper

1. Using a paring knife, cut the broccoli florets from the stem. Cut the florets into 1-inch pieces. Peel and finely chop the stem. Set aside.

2. In a large stockpot, melt the butter over medium-high heat. Sauté the garlic, onion and celery for 2 to 3 minutes or until tender. Stir in the sherry. Add the flour; cook, stirring, until smooth and pale gold, 3 to 5 minutes. Stir in the stock, 1 cup at a time, stirring constantly to remove any flour lumps. Bring to a boil. Reduce heat to low. Stir in the parsley and the broccoli florets and stems. Remove from heat.

3. In a blender or food processor, purée the soup in batches. Return soup to the pot and heat until hot. Whisk in the Cheddar, cream cheese and Parmesan. Season with cayenne, Worcestershire sauce, and nutmeg, and salt and black pepper to taste.

4. Ladle into bowls and garnish with Walnut-Crusted Cheese Balls (see page 76).

Serves 8

Walnut-Crusted Cheese Balls

1/2 cup softened cream cheese

1/2 cup shredded aged Cheddar cheese

2 tbsp. dry sherry

1 green onion, chopped

1 tbsp. chopped fresh thyme

Cayenne pepper

Salt and black pepper

1/2 cup walnut pieces

1. In a food processor, blend the cream cheese, Cheddar and sherry until smooth. Fold in the green onion and thyme. Season to taste with cayenne, salt and black pepper.
2. Form cheese mixture into eight balls. Roll balls in walnut pieces, pressing firmly so the nuts stick to the cheese. Refrigerate for up to 5 days.

Makes 8 balls

Roasted Parsnip and Pear Soup with Goat Cheese and Pistachios

Chef Ned Bell of "Cook Like a Chef Television" made a version of this soup when I judged a fun *Iron Chef* competition at Dish Cooking School in Toronto. Ned won the friendly competition and it was because of this soup.

6 Bosc pears

1 lb. parsnips, cut into 1-inch chunks

1 medium onion, cut into 8 wedges

6 cloves garlic

2 tbsp. olive oil

1 vanilla bean, cut in half lengthwise and seeded

Pinch grated nutmeg

Salt and pepper

2 Yukon Gold potatoes, peeled and diced

8 cups Really Good Roasted Chicken Stock (see page 71)

1 cup heavy cream

Hot sauce to taste

1 1/2 cups crumbled goat cheese

1/4 cup shelled raw pistachio nuts

Honey, for drizzling

1. Preheat oven to 425°F.
2. Peel 4 of the pears. Quarter and core all the pears. In a large bowl, combine the pears, parsnips, onions, garlic, oil, vanilla bean and seeds, and nutmeg. Season to taste with salt and pepper. Stir well. Transfer the mixture to a roasting pan and roast, stirring occasionally, until pears and parsnips are lightly golden but not charred.
3. Transfer the mixture to a large soup pot. Add the potatoes, stock and cream. Bring to a rolling boil. Reduce heat to medium-low and simmer, uncovered and stirring occasionally, for 30 to 40 minutes, until the parsnips and potatoes are very tender. Adjust seasoning with hot sauce, salt and pepper.
4. Ladle into bowls and serve garnished with crumbled goat cheese, pistachios and a drizzle of honey.

Serves 8

Mom's Borscht

My mom is from Latvia, and this is her mother's recipe for borscht. I promise, it's the best you'll ever taste!

2 tbsp. butter

3 cloves garlic, minced

1 medium onion, grated

3 cups grated beets (3 to 4 medium beets fully cooked and peeled)

1 1/2 cups grated cooked carrots (3 to 4 medium carrots)

8 cups Really Good Beef Stock (see page 70)

1 bay leaf

3 cups shredded cabbage

1 tbsp. chopped fresh thyme

1 tbsp. fresh lemon juice

Salt and pepper

8 medium boiled potatoes

1 cup sour cream

1/4 cup chopped flat-leaf parsley

1. In a large soup pot over medium-high heat, melt the butter. Sauté the garlic and onions for 2 to 4 minutes, until transparent and tender. Stir in the beets and carrots; sauté for 2 minutes. Add the stock and bay leaf. Bring to a boil, reduce heat to low and simmer, uncovered and stirring occasionally, for 20 minutes. Stir in the cabbage; simmer for 20 minutes more.
2. Discard the bay leaf. Stir in the thyme and lemon juice, and salt and pepper to taste.
3. Serve with a boiled potato, garnished with a dollop of sour cream and chopped parsley.

Serves 8

Bean Soup with Spam Croutons

Spam croutons! Huh? You can only imagine what I was smoking when I came up with this idea (St. Louis ribs!). But trust me, it is the best garnish for this hearty soup.

6 slices bacon, chopped

4 cloves garlic, minced

1 large onion, diced

1 medium red bell pepper, diced

1 medium green bell pepper, diced

2 jalapeño peppers, diced

3 tbsp. tomato paste

4 cups mixed canned beans (red kidney, navy, black-eyed peas, pinto), rinsed and drained

1 cup store-bought salsa

4 cups Really Good Roasted Chicken Stock (see page 71)

1 to 2 tbsp. Bone Dust BBQ Spice (see page 42)

Dash Worcestershire sauce

Salt and black pepper

2 cups vegetable oil

1 can Spam, cut into 1/2-inch cubes

2 tbsp. chopped fresh cilantro

2 green onions, chopped

2 cups shredded Cheddar cheese

1. In a large soup pot over medium-high heat, sauté the bacon until just crisp. Add the garlic, onion, red pepper, green pepper and jalapeño peppers. Sauté for 3 to 5 minutes until peppers are tender. Stir in the tomato paste, beans, salsa and 3 1/2 cups of the stock. Bring to a boil. Reduce heat to low and simmer, uncovered and stirring occasionally, for 1 hour, adding more stock if necessary to thin. Stir in the Bone Dust BBQ Spice and Worcestershire sauce, and salt and pepper to taste. Set aside, keeping warm.

2. In a separate saucepan, heat the vegetable oil to 350°F. Fry the Spam, in two batches, until crisp, 1 to 2 minutes. Drain on paper towels.

3. Ladle soup into bowls and serve garnished with cilantro, green onions, Cheddar cheese and Spam croutons.

    Serves 8 to 10

Mike's Spicy Seafood Goodness

Chef Mike McColl used to make this soup at Rodney's Oyster Bar and Restaurant in Toronto. I had this spicy seafood goodness many times while eating many an oyster at Rodney's. Mmmmm.

2 tbsp. butter

1 medium red bell pepper, cut into 1/2-inch pieces

1 medium green bell pepper, cut into 1/2-inch pieces

1 Scotch bonnet pepper, minced (include seeds for added heat)

2 medium onions, cut into 1/2-inch pieces

3 stalks celery, cut into 1/2-inch pieces

3 cloves garlic, minced

3 tbsp. curry powder

2 tbsp. minced fresh ginger

1 can (19 oz./540 mL) crushed tomatoes

5 cups Really Good Fish Stock (see page 72)

1 lb. large scallops, cut in quarters

1 lb. shrimp, peeled, deveined and cut in half lengthwise

1 lb. boneless skinless haddock or cod, cut into 2-inch chunks

1/4 cup dark rum

3 tbsp. soy sauce

2 tbsp. lime juice

1 can (12 oz./340 mL) unsweetened coconut milk

2 tbsp. roughly chopped fresh cilantro

Salt and pepper

1. Melt the butter in a medium saucepan over medium-high heat. Add the red pepper, green pepper, Scotch bonnet pepper, onions and celery; sweat for 15 minutes, stirring occasionally. Stir in the garlic, curry powder and ginger; cook for 1 minute. Add the tomatoes and stock. Bring to a boil, reduce heat and simmer for 20 minutes.

2. Meanwhile, in a large bowl, gently stir together the scallops, shrimp, fish, rum, soy sauce and lime juice. Marinate for 15 minutes.

3. Stir the fish and its marinade into the soup. Add the coconut milk and coriander. Simmer for 10 minutes. Season with salt and pepper to taste.

4. Serve with steamed rice.

Serves 8 to 10

Boston Clam Chowder

I have spent a fair amount of time in Boston and have had many bowls of clam chowder—some good and some bad. I believe this recipe, which is loaded with bacon, clams, potatoes and cream, is the best of them all. It is perfect for a cold and damp winter's day.

7 cups 1/2-inch-pieces peeled Yukon Gold potatoes (10 to 12 medium potatoes)

7 cups water

3 tbsp. salt

3 cups homogenized milk

12 slices double-smoked bacon, diced

2 tbsp. butter

2 large red onions, cut in 1/2-inch pieces

2 leeks (white parts only), cut in 1/2-inch pieces

2 cups 1/2-inch pieces celery

3 cans (each 14 oz./398 mL) clams, rinsed and drained OR 1 lb. fresh clam meat

2 cups heavy cream

2 tbsp. soy sauce

1 tsp. dried thyme

Hot sauce to taste

Freshly ground pepper

1. Place the potatoes in a large pot and add the water. Bring to a boil over high heat. Add the salt, reduce heat to medium-low and simmer for 10 minutes or until potatoes are tender. Drain the potatoes, reserving 2 cups of the cooking liquid.

2. In a blender or food processor, purée 2 cups of the potatoes with 1 1/2 cups of the milk. Set aside.

3. Fry the bacon over medium heat until crisp, about 10 minutes. Drain the bacon on paper towels.

4. Add the bacon fat and butter to a large soup pot. Over medium heat, melt the butter. Fry the onions, leeks and celery until tender, 2 to 3 minutes. Cover and steam, stirring occasionally, for 20 minutes or until the vegetables are soft.

5. Add the reserved potato cooking liquid and bring to a boil. Add the potatoes, potato purée, clams, the remaining 1 1/2 cups of milk, the cream, soy sauce, thyme and hot sauce. Bring to a boil.

6. Garnish with freshly ground pepper and serve immediately with crusty bread.

Serves 12

Lobster and Corn Bisque

This soup is best served to the one you love. It is sure to make you feel warm and fuzzy all over.

1 live lobster (2 lb.)

3 tbsp. sea salt

8 cups Really Good Fish Stock (see page 72)

2 tbsp. butter

3 large shallots, diced

3 large Yukon Gold potatoes, peeled and diced

2 cups frozen corn

1 tbsp. chopped fresh thyme

1 tsp. chopped fresh tarragon

2 cups heavy cream

1 cup frozen peas

Salt and pepper

1. In a pot large enough to hold the lobster, add enough water to cover it. Bring water to a boil. Stir in the salt. Plunge lobster head first into the boiling water; return to a boil. Boil lobster for 8 minutes. Remove from pot and let stand until cool enough to touch.

2. Using a large, very sharp knife, slice the lobster from head to tail down the middle. Crack open the claws. Remove tail and claw meat. Cut the meat into 1-inch chunks; set aside. Reserve the lobster shell.

3. Preheat oven to 325°F.

4. Place the lobster shell in a large pot and cover with the fish stock. Bring to a boil over high heat. Reduce heat to low and simmer for 30 minutes. Strain the stock into a bowl; set aside.

5. In the same pot, melt the butter over medium-high heat. Add the shallots, potatoes and corn; sauté for 10 minutes. Add the thyme, tarragon and lobster stock. Bring to a boil, reduce heat and simmer for 30 minutes or until potatoes are tender.

6. In a blender, purée the soup in batches. Strain soup through a fine strainer, discarding any solids.

7. Return the soup to the pot and stir in the cream. Return to a boil; reduce heat and simmer for 10 minutes or until thickened slightly. Stir in the peas and lobster meat; simmer a few minutes, until peas are cooked and lobster is heated through. Season to taste with salt and pepper.

8. Serve with thick and chewy buttered rye bread.

Serves 6 to 8

Chunky Spicy Mexican Chicken Soup

My friend Michael White is a great musician. His band, The White, is the best Led Zeppelin cover band ever. Michael's favourite soup is a Mexican tortilla soup, and the best he has ever had was at Bandito's Mexican Restaurant in Toronto. I tried it and loved it too. Here's my version.

2 lb. plum tomatoes

1/4 cup olive oil

1 lb. boneless skinless chicken breast, cut into 1/2-inch pieces

1 large onion, sliced into 1/2-inch thick rounds

8 cloves garlic, minced

2 stalks celery, cut into 1/2-inch pieces

2 medium carrots, cut into 1/2-inch pieces

1 can (5.5 oz./156 mL) tomato paste

1 or 2 chipotle chilies in adobo sauce, minced

1 can (19 oz./540 mL) chopped tomatoes, drained

1 medium red bell pepper, cut into 1/2-inch pieces

10 cups Really Good Roasted Chicken Stock (see page 71)

1 tbsp. Bone Dust BBQ Spice (see page 42)

1 tbsp. dried oregano

Hot sauce, salt and black pepper to taste

1 avocado, diced

4 limes, halved

1/4 cup chopped fresh cilantro

1 cup sour cream

2 cups shredded Monterey Jack cheese

Tortilla chips, for garnish

1. Preheat grill to high. Grill the plum tomatoes until the skin is blistered and slightly charred. Peel away loose skin and cut tomatoes in half lengthwise. Seed tomatoes and coarsely chop; set aside.

2. In a large soup pot, heat the oil over medium-high heat. Add the chicken and sauté until golden brown. Remove chicken and set aside. Add the onion, garlic, celery and carrots; sauté until tender, 5 to 7 minutes. Stir in the tomato paste and chipotle chilies. Add the charred tomatoes, canned tomatoes, red pepper and stock; bring to a rolling boil. Stir in the Bone Dust BBQ Spice, oregano and reserved chicken. Reduce heat to low and simmer, stirring occasionally, for 40 minutes. Season with hot sauce, salt and black pepper.

3. Ladle soup into bowls. Garnish with avocado, lime, cilantro, sour cream and shredded cheese. Top with crispy tortilla chips.

Serves 8 to 10

Note: To make fresh tortilla crisps, cut flour tortillas into 3- or 4-inch-long thin strips. Fry in 1/2 cup vegetable oil until crisp and golden. Drain on paper towels and season with Bone Dust BBQ Spice.

Sensuous salads with a variety of dressings

Dressings

Salads

Smoked Paprika Sour Cream Dressing

Pan smoking the paprika takes away the bitterness and brings out the nutty, buttery, smoked pepper flavour.

2 tsp. paprika
1/4 cup vegetable oil
1/4 cup sherry vinegar
2 tsp. sugar
1 tsp. dry mustard
1 cup sour cream
Dash chipotle Tabasco sauce
Salt and pepper

1. In a dry small saucepan over high heat, cook the paprika, stirring constantly, for 20 to 30 seconds, until it darkens slightly and turns smoky. This happens quickly, so be careful not to burn the paprika. If it does burn, toss it and start over.
2. Remove from heat and add the oil, vinegar, sugar and mustard; stir until smooth. Return to heat and bring to a low boil. Remove from heat and let cool completely.
3. Stir cooled mixture. Whisk in the sour cream until smooth. Season with a dash of Tabasco, and salt and pepper to taste.
4. Dressing will keep, refrigerated, for up to 1 week.

Makes about 1 1/2 cups

Razzberry Walnut Vinaigrette

Give your salad the "razzberry." This tart and sweet dressing works great with bitter greens, fresh tomatoes and mushrooms.

> 3/4 cup fresh raspberries
>
> 1/4 cup raspberry wine vinegar
>
> 2 tbsp. chopped shallots
>
> 2 tbsp. honey
>
> 2 tbsp. chopped fresh herbs (such as thyme, parsley and tarragon)
>
> 1 tbsp. Dijon mustard
>
> 1/4 cup walnut oil
>
> 2/3 cup vegetable oil
>
> Pinch ground cumin
>
> Salt and pepper

1. In a food processor, blend the raspberries, vinegar, shallots and honey until smooth. Press mixture through a fine sieve to remove seeds. Return to food processor. Add herbs and mustard. With the motor running, add the oils in a steady stream until smooth and well blended. Season to taste with cumin, and salt and pepper to taste.

2. Dressing will keep, refrigerated, for up to 1 week.

Makes about 2 cups

Caramelized Onion and Oka Cheese Ranch Dressing

This dressing also works well with aged white Cheddar cheese. I use the award-winning Canadian Britannia three-year-old.

3/4 cup plus 3 tbsp. vegetable oil

1 large sweet onion, diced

4 cloves garlic, minced

3 egg yolks

1/2 cup sour cream

2 tbsp. cider vinegar

2 tsp. granulated onion (dried onion flakes)

Splash Worcestershire sauce

Dash hot sauce

1 cup shredded Oka cheese

1 tbsp. chopped fresh thyme

Salt and pepper

1. In a large frying pan over medium-high heat, heat 3 tbsp. of the oil. Sauté the onion and garlic, stirring constantly, for 15 to 20 minutes or until the onions are golden brown and sweet. (Caramelizing onions requires patience. You want to extract the sugars from the onion to produce the wonderful golden-brown colour. If you rush it, the onions will char and become bitter.) Let onions cool completely.
2. In a bowl, stir together the onions, egg yolks, sour cream, vinegar, granulated onion, Worcestershire sauce and hot sauce. Gradually stir in the remaining 3/4 cup vegetable oil in a steady stream until fully incorporated. Stir in the cheese and thyme, and salt and pepper to taste.
3. Dressing will keep, refrigerated, for up to 1 week.

Makes about 2 cups

Billy's Woolwich Goat Cheese Vinaigrette

My buddy Billy is a big fan of goat-milk products. He uses Woolwich Dairy's and especially likes its creamy consistency. It's the best as far as I am concerned too.

4 oz. goat cheese (preferably Woolwich), softened

1/4 cup dry white wine

3 tbsp. white wine vinegar

1 egg yolk

1 clove garlic, minced

1 tbsp. chopped fresh herbs (parsley, rosemary, mint, thyme or whatever tickles your fancy)

1/2 tsp. ground fennel

1/2 cup olive oil

Salt and pepper

1. In a bowl, whisk together the goat cheese, wine and vinegar until smooth. Add the egg yolk, garlic, herbs and fennel; whisk until blended. Add the oil in a steady stream, whisking until fully incorporated. Season to taste with salt and pepper.
2. Dressing will keep, refrigerated, for up to 1 week. Serve drizzled over sliced fresh tomatoes or over grilled veal or lamb.

Makes about 1 1/2 cups

Smoked Chipotle Salsa Vinaigrette

This dressing adds zing to any salad. Adjust the spice heat level to suit your tastes. Charring the tomatoes and onion on a grill before chopping them will add a bit of smokiness to the dressing.

3 plum tomatoes, diced

1 small onion, finely diced

1 small green bell pepper, finely diced

1 small red bell pepper, finely diced

1 to 2 small smoked chipotle peppers in adobo sauce, minced

2 cloves garlic, minced

1 cup vegetable oil

1/2 cup white vinegar

1/4 cup chopped fresh cilantro

1/4 cup fresh lime juice

1 tbsp. Mexican Chili Seasoning (see page 45)

2 tsp. sugar

1. In a bowl, whisk together the tomatoes, onion, green pepper, red pepper, chipotle peppers, garlic, oil, vinegar, cilantro, lime juice, Mexican Chili Seasoning and sugar. Let stand for 1 hour before using.
2. Dressing will keep, refrigerated, for up to 1 week. Use to dress salads or as a marinade for fajitas.

Makes about 3 cups

Pucker Up and Smack Me Lemon Vinaigrette

I like to use Meyer lemons for this vinaigrette. Although they are more expensive, they are sweeter than regular lemons and worth the extra cost.

4 cloves garlic, minced
1/2 cup fresh lemon juice
1/2 cup olive oil
1/4 cup chopped shallots
2 tbsp. chopped fresh chives
2 tsp. sugar
1 tsp. lemon zest
1 tsp. dry mustard
1/2 tsp. cracked black pepper
Salt

1. In a bowl, stir together the garlic, lemon juice, oil, shallots, chives, sugar, lemon zest, mustard and pepper. Season to taste with salt.
2. Dressing will keep, refrigerated, for up to 1 week.

Makes about 1 1/4 cups

Pesto Vinaigrette

Pesto vinaigrette is best on pasta salads but it is also a good marinade for fish and poultry.

2 cups basil leaves
4 cloves garlic, chopped
2 tbsp. pine nuts
1/4 cup grated Parmesan cheese
1/4 cup red wine vinegar
1/4 cup olive oil
1 tbsp. lemon juice
Salt and pepper

1. In a food processor, process the basil, garlic and pine nuts until smooth and beginning to form a paste. Add Parmesan cheese, vinegar, olive oil and lemon juice; pulse until fully mixed. Season to taste with salt and pepper.
2. Dressing will keep, refrigerated, for up to 1 week.

Makes about 2 cups

Avocado Ranch Dressing

The Avocado Ranch Rustlers baseball team first made this dressing when they used avocados instead of baseballs to practise with. It seems a well-hit avocado came right out of its skin and flew straight into Granny's glass of buttermilk while she sat on her back porch watching the Rustlers play.

1 avocado, peeled and seeded

2 cloves garlic, minced

3 tbsp. olive oil

2 tbsp. lemon juice

1/2 cup sour cream

1/4 cup buttermilk

3 tbsp. mayonnaise

2 tbsp. water

1 tbsp. white vinegar

1 tbsp. chopped fresh chives

1 tbsp. chopped fresh cilantro

1 tsp. cracked black pepper

1 tsp. dry mustard

Pinch cayenne pepper

Salt to taste

1. In a bowl, mash the avocado. Stir in the garlic, olive oil and lemon juice.
2. In another bowl, whisk together the sour cream, buttermilk, mayonnaise, water and vinegar until smooth. Whisk in the avocado mixture until smooth. Season with the chives, cilantro, mustard, black pepper, cayenne and salt.
3. Dressing will keep, refrigerated, for up to 1 week.

Makes about 2 cups

Lemon Soy Vinaigrette

Chef Mike McColl first made this dressing for me to serve with a sashimi platter of salmon, tuna and barbecued eel.

1 green onion, finely chopped
1 cup fresh lemon juice
1/2 cup soy sauce
1/2 cup rice vinegar
1/2 cup mirin
1 tbsp. chopped fresh cilantro
1 tsp. sesame seeds
1 cup vegetable oil

1. In a bowl, stir together the green onion, lemon juice, soy sauce, vinegar, mirin, cilantro and sesame seeds. Add the oil in a steady stream, whisking until well blended.
2. Dressing will keep, refrigerated, for up to 1 week.

Makes about 3 1/2 cups

Watercress Salad with Lemon Soy Vinaigrette

This is a fast and easy salad that is also light and tasty, with a lot of crunch. Wash the watercress well to remove any grit and the odd bug.

1 cup mandarin orange segments (canned is fine)

2 bunches watercress, thick stems removed

8 radishes, sliced

3 cups bean sprouts

1 cup grated carrot

2 tbsp. toasted sesame seeds

1/4 cup Lemon Soy Vinaigrette (see page 94)

1. In a large bowl, stir together the mandarin oranges, watercress, radishes, bean sprouts and carrots. Sprinkle with the sesame seeds and toss thoroughly.
2. Pour the dressing over the salad and toss thoroughly. Serve immediately.

Serves 6

Popeye's Oriental Spinach Salad

If Popeye's strength came from eating canned spinach alone, just think how much stronger he'd have been after eating this refreshing twist on the classic spinach salad. Toot toot!

Wash the spinach well, making sure you remove all the grit from the leaves. There is nothing worse than eating a spinach salad with sand and grit in it. I usually wash mine twice.

6 slices bacon, diced
6 cups spinach
2 cups bean sprouts
4 large white mushrooms, sliced
1/2 small red onion, thinly sliced
6 radishes, sliced
2 hard-cooked large eggs, diced
1 cup cooked baby shrimp
1/2 cup sliced water chestnuts
2 seedless oranges, peeled and segmented
1/2 cup cashews
1/2 cup Chinese crispy noodles

Wasabi Soy Vinaigrette
1/4 cup vegetable oil
3 tbsp. rice vinegar
2 tbsp. soy sauce
1/2 tsp. toasted sesame seeds
1/2 tsp. wasabi powder
2 tbsp. orange juice
2 tbsp. honey
Pepper to taste
1 tbsp. chopped fresh cilantro

1. In a frying pan, fry the bacon until crisp. Drain on paper towels.
2. In a large bowl, combine the spinach and bean sprouts. In another large bowl, combine the mushrooms, onion, radishes, eggs, shrimp, water chestnuts and bacon. Toss well.
3. Divide spinach among four salad bowls and top with the mushroom mixture. Garnish with orange segments.
4. In a small bowl, whisk together all the vinaigrette ingredients. Drizzle salad with dressing. Garnish with cashews and crispy noodles.

Serves 4

Fire and Ice Spicy Cucumber Salad

Fire is the chili; ice is the cucumber. This salad is a bit like fireworks, accompanied by its very own fire extinguisher.

1 medium English cucumber, peeled, seeded and thinly sliced diagonally

1 small onion, thinly sliced

2 green onions, thinly sliced diagonally

1 stalk celery, finely diced

1, 2 or 3 Thai red chilies, seeded and finely chopped

1/4 cup olive oil

3 tbsp. fresh orange juice

2 tbsp. rice vinegar

2 tsp. sugar

1 tsp. minced fresh ginger

1 tbsp. chopped fresh cilantro

Salt and pepper

1. In a large bowl, combine the cucumber, onion, green onion and celery.
2. In a small saucepan combine the chilies, oil, orange juice, vinegar, sugar and ginger. Bring to a low boil, stirring. Remove from heat and let cool for 5 minutes.
3. Pour over cucumber mixture and stir to mix. Let cool completely. Just before serving, stir in the cilantro. Season to taste with salt and pepper.

Serves 6

Beet Stack with Green Apples and Ermite Blue Cheese with Vanilla Champagne Vinaigrette

This stacked salad is a little more work than just tossing in a bowl, but the presentation is eye popping. See the picture that appears after page 52.

4 large beets
1 vanilla bean, split and seeded, reserving seeds
2 tsp. sugar
1 tsp. salt
1/4 cup champagne
1/4 cup champagne vinegar
2 tbsp. chopped fresh thyme
1 tbsp. honey
1 tbsp. Dijon mustard
1/2 cup olive oil
Salt and pepper
2 Granny Smith apples
2 tbsp. lemon juice
2 medium shallots, thinly sliced
1 green onion, thinly sliced
1 tbsp. prepared horseradish OR freshly grated horseradish
1/4 cup crumbled Canadian Ermite blue cheese or Stilton or Roquefort blue cheese
1 bunch arugula
1 pint onion sprouts
8 pieces shaved Canadian Ermite blue cheese or Stilton or Roquefort blue cheese

1. Place beets, scraped vanilla bean, sugar and salt in a large saucepan; cover with water. Bring to a boil; reduce heat to medium low and simmer for 30 to 40 minutes, until the beets are just tender. Remove from heat and let beets stand in cooking liquid for 1 hour.

2. Remove beets from cooking liquid. Strain cooking liquid into a bowl and set aside. Under cool running water, peel the beets. Return beets to cooking liquid. Set aside.

3. In a bowl, whisk together the vanilla seeds, champagne, champagne vinegar, 1 tbsp. of the thyme, the honey and mustard. Add the oil in a steady stream, whisking constantly until well blended. Season to taste with salt and pepper. Set vinaigrette aside.

4. Cut the top and bottom off each apple. Core the apples with an apple corer. Cut the apples crosswise into 1/4-inch-thick slices. Cut each slice into matchstick-sized pieces. Transfer apples to a bowl and toss gently with the lemon juice. Add the shallots, green onion, horseradish, remaining 1 tbsp. thyme, and salt and pepper to taste. Gently stir. Add the crumbled cheese and 1/4 cup of the vanilla champagne vinaigrette. Gently stir.

5. In a large bowl, toss the arugula and onion sprouts with 3 tbsp. of the vinaigrette.

6. Remove beets from cooking liquid (discarding liquid) and cut beets crosswise into twelve 1/2-inch-thick slices; season to taste with salt and pepper.

7. Place a beet slice in the centre of each of four salad plates. Top beet slices with half of the apple mixture. Top with a second beet slice. Top with the remaining apple mixture and the remaining beet slices.

8. Top each beet stack with a small handful of the arugula mixture. Garnish each stack with 2 slices of shaved cheese. Drizzle each salad with 1 to 2 tbsp. of the vinaigrette. Serve immediately.

Serves 4

Chop Chop Cobb Salad with Avocado Ranch Dressing

All the knife work for this salad is well worth it. Chop chop and have fun.

3 boneless skinless chicken breasts

1 to 2 tbsp. Bone Dust BBQ Spice (see page 42)

1/2 cup your favourite BBQ sauce

3 slices smoked back bacon

1 small head iceberg lettuce

1 head radicchio, cut into 1 1/2-inch pieces

2 cups curly endive leaves

1 cup Avocado Ranch Dressing (see page 93), plus additional for drizzling

4 hard-cooked eggs, chopped

2 large ripe beefsteak tomatoes, coarsely chopped

2 small red onions, chopped

2 ripe avocados, diced and tossed in 1 tbsp. lemon juice

1 English cucumber, peeled and chopped

1 cup seasoned store-bought croutons

2 roasted red bell peppers, peeled, seeded and chopped

1 cup crumbled Canadian Ermite or other blue cheese

1. Preheat grill to medium-high.
2. Season chicken with Bone Dust BBQ Spice, rubbing the spices into the meat. Grill chicken for 5 minutes; turn and baste with BBQ sauce. Grill another 5 to 6 minutes, or until well done. Chill the chicken.
3. Meanwhile, grill the bacon for 2 to 3 minutes per side. Chill the bacon.
4. Core the iceberg lettuce by giving the head a firm smack on the counter. Twist core to remove. Hold the lettuce under cold running water and fill the cavity with water. Drain well and chop. In a large bowl, toss the iceberg lettuce, radicchio and endive with the Avocado Ranch Dressing. Arrange on a large serving platter.
5. Thinly slice chicken and lay across the lettuces in a straight line. Cube the bacon and arrange beside chicken.
6. Next to the meats, arrange a row each of chopped egg, tomatoes, red onions, avocados, cucumber, croutons and roasted peppers. Sprinkle with cheese, drizzle with extra dressing and serve.

Serves 4

Mrs. Jacobson's Potato Salad with Olives

My mother-in-law, Carole, makes a killer potato salad. You are sure to find it at any Jacobson family barbecue, at which I always seem to be cooking. It's summer in a bowl!

6 medium unpeeled Yukon Gold potatoes

1 stalk celery, sliced

1 small onion, diced

2 green onions, thinly sliced

2 hard-cooked eggs, diced

12 green pimento-stuffed olives, sliced

2 tbsp. prepared mustard

3/4 cup Miracle Whip salad dressing

Salt and pepper

1. In a large pot, boil the potatoes in salted water until just tender, 30 to 40 minutes. Drain potatoes and cut into bite-sized chunks.
2. In a large bowl, combine the potatoes, celery, onion, green onions, eggs, olives, mustard and salad dressing. Stir well. Season with salt and pepper to taste.
3. For best results, refrigerate overnight.

Serves 6 to 8

Mom's Warm Marinated Carrot Salad

This great salad can be served cold as a refreshing summer salad or warm as a side dish.

2 lb. carrots, sliced into 1/2-inch rounds

1 small green bell pepper, cut into strips

1 large onion, sliced into rings

Marinade

1 cup Really Good Tomato Sauce (see page 73)

1/2 cup sugar

1/2 cup cider vinegar

1/2 cup vegetable oil

1 tsp. celery seeds

1 tsp. dry mustard

Salt and pepper

1. Cook carrots in boiling salted water for 6 to 8 minutes or until tender; drain well. Combine carrots, peppers and onion and set aside.
2. In a small saucepan, combine the tomato sauce, sugar, vinegar, oil, celery seeds, mustard, salt and pepper. Stir over medium heat until well mixed and heated through. Pour over carrot mixture and stir well.
3. To serve warm, transfer salad to a casserole dish. Bake, covered, at 350°F for 20 minutes or until warmed through.
4. To serve cold, refrigerate, covered, for 4 to 6 hours.

Serves 8

Asparagus Salad with Prosciutto, Goat Cheese and Roasted Red Pepper

When shopping for asparagus, look for tender young stalks, which have the sweetest flavour. If you can find only thick-stemmed asparagus, peel the stalks so they will not be as woody tasting.

2 lb. asparagus, trimmed

4 tbsp. sherry vinegar

1 tsp. salt

1 large shallot, diced

2 tbsp. medium-dry sherry

1 tbsp. chopped fresh lemon thyme

1 tbsp. Dijon mustard

1/3 cup olive oil

Salt and pepper

4 slices prosciutto, cut into thin strips

1 roasted red bell pepper, peeled, seeded and thinly sliced

1/2 cup crumbled goat cheese

1. Bring a large pot of water to a boil. Add asparagus, 1 tbsp. of the sherry vinegar and 1 tsp. salt. Boil until asparagus is bright green, about 2 minutes. Be careful not to overcook your asparagus. Drain and rinse under cold water to cool completely. Pat dry on paper towels and set aside.

2. In a bowl, whisk together the shallot, the remaining 3 tbsp. sherry vinegar, the sherry, thyme and Dijon. Add the oil in a steady stream, whisking until fully incorporated. Season to taste with salt and pepper.

3. Arrange the asparagus on a platter. Sprinkle with the prosciutto, red pepper and goat cheese. Drizzle with dressing. Serve immediately.

Serves 6

Bursting Baby Grape Tomato and Baby Bocconcini Salad

Buy the smallest bocconcini balls you can find—one-bite balls make this salad the best. You'll have exploding juicy tomatoes with the soft bite of marinated bocconcini.

12 balls baby bocconcini OR fresh mozzarella balls, halved or quartered

2 dill cucumbers, cut into 1/2-inch chunks

1 medium shallot, finely chopped

1 pint grape tomatoes, halved if large

2 tbsp. roasted garlic, minced (see page 221)

2 tbsp. chopped fresh herbs (such as basil, oregano and flat-leaf parsley)

2 tbsp. olive oil

2 splashes balsamic vinegar

Honey to taste

Salt and pepper

1. In a large bowl, combine the bocconcini, cucumbers, shallot, tomatoes, garlic and herbs.
2. Drizzle olive oil, balsamic vinegar and honey over tomatoes. Season to taste with salt and pepper. Stir well.
3. Marinate at room temperature for 1 hour before serving.

Serves 6

Lobster Avocado Salad

This recipe is a collaboration between my mom and me. It's her lobster salad, jazzed up by my addition of avocado, jalapeño and cilantro. This salad also makes a great filling for sandwiches. I like to make lobster club sandwiches by topping toasted challah with Lobster Avocado Salad, crispy fried thick-sliced pepper bacon, vine-ripened tomatoes and butter lettuce. Serve with champagne and you have a wonderful brunch.

3 large avocados

Juice of 1 lime

1 lb. chilled cooked lobster meat (thawed and drained well if using frozen)

2 green onions, thinly sliced diagonally

1 small green bell pepper, diced

1 small red bell pepper, diced

1 jalapeño pepper, seeded and finely chopped

1/2 cup diced onion

1/2 cup mayonnaise

2 tbsp. chopped fresh cilantro

1 tsp. Bone Dust BBQ Spice (see page 42)

Dash chipotle Tabasco sauce

Salt and freshly ground black pepper

1. Cut the avocados in half and remove the seeds. Scoop out a larger hole in the avocados, leaving a 1/2-inch rim, and transferring avocado flesh to a large bowl. Rub avocado "bowls" with some of the lime juice and cover with plastic. Refrigerate until needed.
2. To the avocado, add the remaining lime juice, the lobster meat, green onions, green pepper, red pepper, jalapeño pepper, onion, mayonnaise, cilantro and Bone Dust BBQ Spice. Season with a dash of Tabasco, and salt and black pepper to taste. Stir well. Cover and chill for 1 hour.
3. Serve in the avocado bowls.

Serves 6

Melon Shrimp Salad

The melon shrimp salad is the No. 1–selling salad at the local diner in Melonville. This is my version. It won the Best Salad award at the Melonville Melon Awards Recipe Competition.

1 cantaloupe

1 honeydew melon

1 small seedless watermelon

4 cups water

2 tbsp. Bone Dust BBQ Spice (see page 42)

Dash hot sauce

1 lime, thinly sliced

1 lb. extra-large shrimp (16–20/lb. count), peeled and deveined

1 green bell pepper, finely diced

1 jalapeño pepper, finely diced

1/4 cup chopped shallots

1/4 cup olive oil

1/4 cup orange juice

1 tbsp. chopped Thai basil

1 tbsp. chopped fresh cilantro

1 tbsp. Grand Marnier

Bone Dust BBQ Spice, salt and black pepper

1. Cut each melon in half. Using a melon baller, scoop uniform balls from the melons, transferring balls to a big bowl. Cover and refrigerate. (Now you will have a lot of extra melon flesh hanging around, so eat it as you cook, make a shake or juice it. It's refreshing and good for you.)
2. In a large saucepan, bring the water, Bone Dust BBQ Spice, hot sauce and lime to a boil. Add the shrimp and return to a boil. Poach shrimp for 3 to 5 minutes, until shrimp are opaque and just cooked through. Drain and let cool.
3. Cut each shrimp in half lengthwise. Add to melon balls along with green pepper, jalapeño pepper, shallots, oil, orange juice, Thai basil, cilantro and Grand Marnier. Toss well. Season to taste with Bone Dust, salt and black pepper.
4. Chill for at least 1 hour before serving.

Serves 8

Shrimp and Vegetable Salad with Pucker Up and Smack Me Lemon Vinaigrette

Use lots of shrimp in this salad. The more, the tastier. It's a summertime favourite at my backyard BBQ parties.

2 lb. asparagus, trimmed

1 lb. green beans, trimmed

1 cup sugar snap peas

1 medium yellow bell pepper, sliced

1 large red onion, sliced

4 green onions, thinly sliced

1/2 cup niçoise olives

2 tbsp. chopped fresh dill

1 tbsp. capers

1/3 cup Pucker Up and Smack Me Lemon Vinaigrette (see page 91)

1 lb. chilled (or thawed frozen) cooked extra-large shrimp (16–20/lb. count), peeled and deveined

Salt and freshly ground black pepper

1. Cut the asparagus, green beans and snap peas diagonally into 2-inch lengths. Bring a large pot of water to a boil. Blanch the asparagus, beans and peas for 2 minutes, until just tender. Drain and cool under running cold water. Drain again.

2. In a large bowl, combine the shrimp, asparagus, beans, sugar peas, yellow pepper, red onion, green onions, olives, dill, capers and vinaigrette. Gently toss to thoroughly coat all ingredients. Season to taste with salt and pepper.

3. Cover and refrigerate for 1 hour to allow all the flavours to develop. Remove from refrigerator 20 minutes before serving. Serve with warm crusty bread.

Serves 8

Toasted Orzo Salad with Asiago Cheese and Grape Tomatoes

My Chef Mike McColl created this recipe. He says "toasted anything almost always tastes better." Toasting the orzo in a dry pan brings out a nuttier flavour and will also enhance your salad's appearance.

1 1/2 cups orzo
2 tsp. Bone Dust BBQ Spice (see page 42)
1 tsp. salt
3 tbsp. olive oil
2 cooked chicken breasts, diced
1 pint grape tomatoes, halved
1 medium onion, diced
2 green onions, chopped
1 cup shredded Asiago cheese
1/4 cup diced black olives
2 tbsp. chopped fresh herbs
1/2 cup Pesto Vinaigrette (see page 92)
Salt and pepper
2 tbsp. pine nuts

1. In a large nonstick frying pan over high heat, toast the orzo, stirring constantly, until the pasta is light golden brown and has a slightly nutty flavour, 1 to 2 minutes.
2. Bring a large pot of water to a boil. Stir in the orzo, Bone Dust BBQ Spice and 1 tsp. salt. Cook pasta for 6 to 8 minutes or until al dente. Drain orzo and transfer to a large bowl. Stir in olive oil and let cool.
3. Add chicken, tomatoes, onion, green onions, Asiago cheese, olives, herbs and pesto vinaigrette. Toss well. Season to taste with salt and pepper. Serve garnished with pine nuts.

Serves 6 to 8

Colonel Mustard's Slaw

Colonel Mustard did it to the cabbage, in the kitchen, with the knife. But who did Miss Scarlet do?

1/2 head cabbage, thinly sliced
4 leaves mustard greens, thinly sliced
1 medium yellow bell pepper, thinly sliced
1 medium red onion, thinly sliced
3 green onions, thinly sliced
1 cup grated carrots
2 tbsp. chopped fresh parsley
1/2 cup vegetable oil
1/2 cup malt vinegar
2 tbsp. Dijon mustard
1 tbsp. dry mustard
1 tbsp. chopped fresh tarragon
1 tbsp. brown sugar
1 tsp. yellow mustard seeds
1 tsp. black mustard seeds
Salt and pepper

1. In a large bowl, combine the cabbage, mustard greens, yellow pepper, red onion, green onions, carrots and parsley.
2. In a small saucepan, stir together the oil, vinegar, Dijon mustard, dry mustard, tarragon, sugar, yellow mustard seeds and black mustard seeds. Bring to a low boil and simmer, stirring occasionally, for 5 minutes. Pour over the cabbage mixture. Toss to coat evenly. Season to taste with salt and pepper.
3. Marinate, covered and refrigerated, for 2 hours before serving.

Serves 6 to 8

Monterey Mexican Jicama Slaw

Whenever Mike and I consumed vast quantities of tequila in Mexico while working the CART racing circuit, we ate this salad at a bar or two … I think? I know there was lots of tequila.

1 jicama, peeled and julienned

1 seedless cucumber, peeled and julienned

1 large carrot, julienned

1 small onion, thinly sliced

1 tbsp. chopped fresh cilantro

Juice of 1 lime

1/4 cup olive oil

1/4 cup fresh orange juice

1 tbsp. Bayou Bite Cajun Rub (see page 44)

Pinch sugar

Salt and pepper

1. In a large bowl, combine the jicama, cucumber, carrot, onion and cilantro.
2. In a small bowl, whisk together lime juice, orange juice, oil, Bayou Bite Cajun Rub and sugar. Pour over jicama mixture and toss well. Season to taste with salt and pepper. Serve dusted with extra Cajun Rub.

Serves 6 to 8

Fennel Pancetta Slaw

This salad is great with grilled lamb chops or oven-roasted lamb ribs.

2 bulbs fennel, cored and very thinly sliced

1 medium red onion, thinly sliced

3 green onions, thinly sliced diagonally

1 medium yellow banana pepper, finely diced

1 cubanelle pepper, julienned

2 tbsp. chopped fresh basil

3 tbsp. olive oil

3 tbsp. white grape juice

3 tbsp. white wine vinegar

4 tsp. dry mustard

Salt and pepper

8 slices pancetta

1 tbsp. chopped fresh parsley

1 tbsp. chopped fresh thyme

1 tsp. poppy seeds or black mustard seeds

1. In a large bowl, combine the fennel, red onion, green onions, banana pepper, cubanelle pepper and basil.
2. In a small bowl, whisk together the oil, grape juice, vinegar and 2 tsp. of the dry mustard. Season to taste with salt and pepper. Pour over fennel mixture. Cover and refrigerate for 1 hour.
3. In a frying pan over medium-high heat, fry the pancetta for 1 to 3 minutes per side or until crisp. Remove from pan and pat excess oil from pancetta with paper towels. Thinly slice pancetta.
4. Add pancetta, parsley, thyme, poppy seeds and remaining 2 tsp. dry mustard to fennel; toss. Serve immediately.

Serves 6 to 8

Just like mamma used to make: pasta, polenta and more

Scoobi Doo Pasta Carbonara with Tons of Bacon and Onions

Scoobi doo pasta, also known as double elbow or twisted macaroni, is fun pasta. It's got lots of room, inside and out, to cradle this succulent carbonara sauce.

2 large egg yolks

1/3 cup heavy cream

1 lb. scoobi doo pasta

8 slices thick-cut double-smoked bacon, diced

4 cloves garlic, minced

1 medium red onion, sliced

1 1/2 cups sliced white mushrooms

Salt and freshly ground black pepper

2 tbsp. chopped fresh basil

1/4 cup grated Parmesan cheese

1. In a medium bowl, whisk together egg yolks and cream. Set aside.
2. In a large pot of boiling salted water, cook pasta until al dente. Stir it occasionally so the pasta doesn't stick, because scrubbing a pot with pasta stuck on the bottom sucks. Drain well.
3. Meanwhile, cook the bacon in a medium saucepan over medium-high heat until crisp. Drain excess fat. Add the garlic and onion; sauté for 3 to 5 minutes, until onion is tender and slightly golden brown. Add the mushrooms and cook until the mushrooms are tender and most of the moisture has evaporated.
4. Add the drained pasta to the pan. Reduce heat to medium and add the egg mixture. Stir and gently heat until the sauce is thick, being careful not to boil the egg mixture or the egg will scramble. Remove from heat and stir in basil. Season to taste with salt and pepper.
5. Serve immediately, sprinkled with Parmesan cheese.

Serves 4 as a main course (or 6 as an appetizer)

Scallop and Shrimp Linguine Toss

This is one of my sister-in-law Sigal's favourite dishes. It's got all of her favourite things served conveniently in one bowl. She could eat this dish every time she comes over for dinner, if only I would let her.

1 lb. linguine

1 lb. extra-large tiger shrimp (16–20/lb. count), peeled and deveined

1 lb. large scallops

1 tbsp. Bone Dust BBQ Spice (see page 42)

4 tbsp. olive oil

1 long thin red chili, minced

1 small sweet onion, very thinly sliced

1/2 cup thinly sliced roasted red bell pepper

1 cup Really Good Tomato Sauce (see page 73)

1/4 cup white wine

Salt and black pepper

1/4 cup grated Romano cheese

Squeeze lemon juice

1. Cook linguine in a large pot of boiling salted water until al dente. Stir it occasionally so the pasta doesn't stick, because scrubbing a pot with pasta stuck on the bottom sucks. Drain well.
2. Season shrimp and scallops with Bone Dust BBQ Spice. In a large frying pan over medium-high heat, heat 2 tbsp. of the olive oil. Add the shrimp and scallops and cook for 1 minute per side or until scallops are seared on each side and shrimp just turn pink. Remove from pan and set aside.
3. In the same pan, heat the remaining 2 tbsp. of oil. Add the chili, onion and roasted red pepper; sauté for 2 minutes or until tender. Stir in the tomato sauce and wine. Bring to a boil. Add the shrimp, scallops and drained pasta; toss well to coat. Season to taste with salt and pepper.
4. Divide among four pasta bowls. Serve immediately, garnished with Romano cheese and a squeeze of fresh lemon.

Serves 4

Lotsa Clams Marinara

The more clams you put in this, the better it gets. I once made this for CART racing's team owner, Derrick Walker, for lunch. Derrick seldom has seconds. That lunch, he had two huge bowls.

1 tbsp. butter

6 cloves garlic, minced

1 small onion, thinly sliced

3 to 4 lb. fresh littleneck clams, rinsed well

1/2 cup dry white wine

1 lb. linguine

2 cups Really Good Tomato Sauce (see page 73)

Salt and pepper

1/4 cup chopped fresh basil

1. In a large pot melt the butter over medium-high heat. Add the garlic and onion and sauté for 2 minutes. Add the clams and wine. Cover and bring to a boil over high heat. Reduce heat to medium-high and steam the clams for 6 to 8 minutes or until most of the clams have opened. Using a slotted spoon, transfer the open clams to a bowl. Continue to steam any clams that have not opened. Transfer the opened clams to the bowl and discard any clams that did not open. Set aside 12 clams in their shells for garnish, and remove clam meat from the remaining shells.

2. Meanwhile, cook linguine in a large pot of boiling salted water until al dente. Stir it occasionally so the pasta doesn't stick, because scrubbing a pot with pasta stuck on the bottom sucks. Drain well.

3. Add the Really Good Tomato Sauce to the clam pot and bring to a boil. Reduce heat to medium and reduce the sauce slightly. Add the clam meat and the pasta. Toss well to coat. Season to taste with salt and pepper.

4. Divide the pasta among four pasta bowls and garnish with the clams in the shell and chopped basil. Serve immediately with toasted garlic bread.

Serves 4

Drunken Chicken BBQ Sundaes (page 29)

Lobster and Corn Bisque (page 82)

Three-Meat Lasagna with Old School Garlic Bread

I'm not Italian nor am I normal, so I never make anything like a normal Italian would make. There's always a twist. I use three varieties of ground meat and a ton of cheese in my lasagna. According to my Italian bellissima, Rosi, "this recipe rocks." Not as good as her mamma's, but it still rocks.

1 lb. ground veal

1 lb. ground pork

1 lb. ground beef

8 cloves garlic, minced

1 tbsp. crumbled dried basil

1 tbsp. Bone Dust BBQ Spice (see page 42)

Salt and pepper to taste

4 slices bacon, chopped

2 1/2 cups Really Good Tomato Sauce (see page 73)

2 cups firm ricotta cheese

2 cups grated mozzarella cheese

1 cup grated Asiago cheese

2 cups grated Parmesan cheese

1/4 cup olive oil

1 cup dry bread crumbs

1 tbsp. chopped fresh basil

1 tbsp. parsley

6 to 8 fresh lasagna noodles (about 8 × 4 inches)

1. In a large bowl, combine the veal, pork, beef, garlic, dried basil, Bone Dust BBQ Spice, salt and pepper. Mix thoroughly.
2. In a large frying pan, sauté the bacon until crisp. Transfer the bacon to a bowl. In the bacon fat, fry the meat mixture in batches, stirring frequently, until fully cooked, adding meat as cooked to the bacon.
3. Return the meat and the bacon to the frying pan, add the tomato sauce and bring to a boil, stirring occasionally. Reduce heat to low and simmer, uncovered and stirring occasionally, for 30 to 40 minutes or until meat is tender and sauce is quite thick but still saucy. Let cool completely.
4. Preheat oven to 375°F. Place two 11 × 8 1/2-inch foil lasagna pans one inside the other and line the top pan with nonstick foil.

5. In a bowl, stir together the ricotta, mozzarella, Asiago and 1 cup of the Parmesan cheese until blended. In another bowl, stir together the olive oil, remaining 1 cup of Parmesan cheese, the bread crumbs, basil, parsley and salt to taste.

6. Make a single layer of lasagna noodles in the pan. Spread with one third of the tomato sauce. Spread with one third of the cheese mixture. Make another layer of lasagna sheets. Repeat layers of sauce, cheese and pasta. Cover with nonstick foil.

7. Bake for 45 to 50 minutes or until heated through and the cheese is melted. Remove foil and sprinkle with bread crumb mixture. Continue to bake for a few minutes until the top is golden brown. Let stand for 10 to 15 minutes.

8. Turn out onto a platter or portion straight from the pan. Serve with heated tomato sauce, Old School Garlic Bread (see page 224) and good wine.

Serves 6

No-Lie Pinocchio Meataballs and Spaghetti

Justa likea Mamma used to make. Bigga juicy meataballs with loads of garlic, smothered in tomato sauce. Wear a bib and start drooling.

3 lb. ground chuck

1 large onion, diced

8 cloves garlic, minced

Salt and pepper to taste

3 cups white button mushrooms, quartered

2 medium onions, sliced

2 medium roasted red bell peppers, peeled, seeded and chopped

1 tbsp. crushed red chilies

1 can (5.5 oz./156 mL) tomato paste

4 cups Really Good Tomato Sauce (see page 73)

1/2 cup water

2 tbsp. balsamic vinegar

1 lb. spaghetti

2 tbsp. olive oil

1 cup torn fresh basil leaves

1/4 cup grated Romano cheese, plus extra for sprinkling

Salt, pepper and crushed red chilies to taste

1. In a large bowl, combine the ground chuck, diced onion, garlic, salt and pepper. Using your hands, mix well. Cover and refrigerate for 30 minutes to allow the flavours to develop.
2. Line a tray with plastic wrap. Form meat into large balls—big ones, baby, like tennis balls! Place meatballs on the tray and refrigerate, covered, for another 30 minutes.
3. Preheat oven to 300°F.
4. Spray a large, heavy frying pan with nonstick cooking spray and heat over medium-high heat. Add meatballs in batches, being careful not to overcrowd the pan. Brown the meatballs on all sides, turning frequently. Transfer browned meatballs to a roasting pan.
5. In the same pan, sauté the mushrooms until tender and lightly browned. Stir in sliced onions, roasted peppers and crushed chilies. Stir in tomato paste, Really Good Tomato Sauce, water and balsamic vinegar.
6. Pour sauce over meatballs. Cover roasting pan tightly with foil and bake for 2 hours, stirring gently occasionally. Uncover and bake for 1 hour.
7. About 15 minutes before the meatballs are ready, cook spaghetti in a large pot of boiling salted water until al dente. Drain well.
8. Toss pasta in the cooking pot with olive oil, basil, Romano cheese, salt, pepper and crushed chilies. Transfer to a serving bowl. Add sauce and meatballs. Sprinkle with additional Romano cheese.
9. Now that's a spicy meatball!

Serves 6 to 8

Smoked Ham, Macaroni and Cheese Bake

This is ooey, gooey, messy, mouthwatering, belly-filling goodness. Kids love it, and it beats KD. Now it's KQ.

1 lb. double elbow macaroni (scoobi doo pasta)
4 large eggs
3 cups shredded white Cheddar cheese
1 can (14 oz./398 mL) evaporated milk
3/4 cup butter, softened
2 tsp. Bone Dust BBQ Spice (see page 42)
Salt
2 cups diced smoked ham
1 1/2 cups cubed Velveeta cheese
1 cup green peas
2 cups coarsely crushed regular potato chips
1/2 cup grated Parmesan cheese
2 tbsp. chopped fresh parsley
Black pepper to taste

1. Preheat oven to 350°F. Butter a 12 × 8-inch casserole dish.
2. In a large pot of boiling salted water, cook pasta until al dente. Stir it occasionally so the pasta doesn't stick, because scrubbing a pot with pasta stuck on the bottom sucks. Drain well.
3. While the pasta cooks, in a medium bowl, lightly beat the eggs. Stir in the cheddar cheese and evaporated milk.
4. Return drained pasta to the pot over low heat. Add butter and the egg mixture. Stir for 2 to 3 minutes or until cheese and butter melt and the mixture is saucy but not too thick. Add more milk if necessary. Remove from heat.
5. Stir in Bone Dust BBQ Spice and salt to taste. Stir in ham, Velveeta cheese and peas. Evenly spread mixture in casserole dish. Cover with foil. Bake for 30 minutes.
6. Combine potato chips, Parmesan cheese, parsley and black pepper. Spread chip mixture over macaroni and cheese. Cook, uncovered, for another 15 minutes , until all is golden, crispy, ooey and gooey. Let cool for at least 5 minutes. Serve hot.

Serves 8

Chicken Penne Bake with Fontina Custard

The creamy custard cheese topping makes this pasta a real treat. Loaded with ground chicken and fontina cheese, it's a great winter warming pasta.

1 lb. ground chicken

1 tbsp. Bone Dust BBQ Spice (see page 42)

Salt and pepper to taste

5 tbsp. olive oil

1 large onion, sliced

4 cloves garlic, minced

3 cups Really Good Tomato Sauce (see page 73)

2 cups sliced mushrooms

1 lb. penne

2 cups cubed fontina cheese

3 eggs

1 cup ricotta cheese

1 cup grated fontina cheese

3/4 cup heavy cream

1 tbsp. chopped fresh herbs (such as basil, oregano, rosemary, parsley)

1. Preheat oven to 375°F. Butter a deep 12 × 8-inch casserole dish.
2. In a bowl, season chicken with Bone Dust BBQ Spice, salt and pepper. Mix well.
3. In a large frying pan, heat 3 tbsp. of the olive oil over high heat. Fry the ground chicken, in batches, until fully cooked, transferring chicken as cooked to a bowl. Drain fat from pan.
4. In the same pan, heat the remaining 2 tbsp. of olive oil. Sauté the onions, garlic and mushrooms for 8 to 10 minutes, until lightly browned and there is no moisture in the pan. Add chicken and 2 cups of Really Good Tomato Sauce. Bring to a boil, reduce heat and simmer for 5 minutes. Set aside.
5. In a large pot of boiling salted water, cook penne until al dente. Stir it occasionally so the pasta doesn't stick, because scrubbing a pot with pasta stuck on the bottom sucks. Drain well.
6. In large bowl, stir together penne, chicken mixture and remaining 1 cup of Really Good Tomato Sauce. The mixture should be moist but not too runny; add a little extra tomato sauce if the mixture looks too dry. Add cubed fontina cheese and mix well. Season to taste with salt and pepper. Pour mixture into casserole dish.
7. In a medium bowl, beat the eggs. Whisk in the ricotta cheese, grated fontina cheese, cream, herbs and salt to taste until smooth. Pour over penne mixture.
8. Bake, uncovered, for 40 to 45 minutes or until the top is golden brown and set. Let rest for 5 to 10 minutes. Serve hot.

Serves 6 to 8

Risotto with Sweet Peas, Shrimp and More Shrimp

Risotto is a meal in itself, great as an appetizer but so much better as a main course. Lots of little shrimp, and some big shrimp too, make this rice dish succulent.

Risotto

5 cups Really Good Roasted Chicken Stock (see page 71)

2 tbsp. butter

1 tbsp. olive oil

1 small onion, finely diced

2 cloves garlic, minced

1 1/2 cups Arborio rice

1 cup Chardonnay or other dry white wine

Salt and pepper

Shrimp

12 extra-large shrimp (16–20/lb. count), peeled and deveined

1 tbsp. Bone Dust BBQ Spice (see page 42)

1 tbsp. olive oil

2 tbsp. butter

4 cloves garlic, minced

1 small red onion, diced

2 cups cooked baby shrimp

1 medium roasted red bell pepper, thinly sliced

1 cup sweet peas

1 1/2 cups Really Good Tomato Sauce (see page 73)

1/2 cup chopped green onions

2 tbsp. grated Parmesan cheese

1 tbsp. chopped fresh herbs (such as oregano, basil, thyme)

Salt and pepper

1. To make the risotto, bring the stock to a simmer. In a large, heavy saucepan, melt the butter and oil over medium heat. Add the onions and garlic; cook, stirring, for 3 to 5 minutes, until the onions are tender. Stir in the rice and cook for a minute or so until the rice is coated with the oil. Add the wine, stirring until most of the wine is absorbed. Add the hot stock, 1 cup at a time, stirring slowly and constantly and allowing the rice to absorb all the liquid before adding more. Keep stirring until all of the stock is absorbed and the rice is creamy and tender, about 20 to 25 minutes. Season to taste with salt and pepper. Set aside, keeping warm.

2. In a large bowl, toss the raw shrimp with the Bone Dust BBQ Spice and oil

3. In a large, heavy frying pan, melt the butter over medium-high heat. Sauté the garlic and onions for 2 minutes or until tender. Add the raw shrimp and fry for 3 to 5 minutes, turning, until shrimp are tender and opaque. Add baby shrimp, roasted pepper, peas and Really Good Tomato Sauce. Boil for 1 minute. Pour over risotto and stir to combine. Stir in green onions, Parmesan cheese, herbs, and salt and pepper to taste. Serve immediately.

Serves 6

Pad Thai with Chicken and Shrimp

The Bamboo Nightclub in Toronto was famous for its pad thai, which was absolutely delicious. It was a must-have before and after any concert at the Bamboo! This version is equally good.

1 lb. pad thai rice noodles

1/4 cup + 2 tbsp. vegetable oil

1/2 lb. boneless skinless chicken breasts, thinly sliced crosswise

1 lb. large shrimp (21–30/lb. count), peeled and deveined

1 medium red bell pepper, diced

1 small red onion, thinly sliced

2 cloves garlic, minced

1/4 cup Really Good Roasted Chicken Stock (see page 71)

1/4 cup ketchup

1/4 cup soy sauce

2 tbsp. rice wine vinegar

2 tsp. sugar

1 tsp. sambal oelek

Dash Asian fish sauce

3 green onions, chopped

2 tbsp. chopped fresh cilantro

2 cups bean sprouts

1/2 cup crushed peanuts

1. Place noodles in a large bowl. Cover with boiling water and soak until tender but still firm to the bite, 6 to 8 minutes. Drain and set aside.
2. Heat 2 tbsp. of the oil in a large frying pan over high heat. Add the chicken strips and stir-fry for 2 minutes. Add the shrimp; stir-fry for 3 minutes or until the chicken and shrimp are just cooked. Transfer chicken and shrimp to a bowl and set aside.
3. Reduce the heat to medium-high and add the red peppers and onion to the pan; stir-fry for 3 minutes. Add the garlic; stir-fry for 1 minute. Add mixture to chicken.
4. Add remaining 1/4 cup of oil to the pan and heat over medium-high. Add noodles and fry, without stirring, for 3 to 5 minutes, until the noodles are lightly browned and crisp on one side. Stir noodles, then stir in the chicken stock, ketchup, soy sauce, vinegar, sugar, sambal oelek and fish sauce. Bring to a boil. Stir in the chicken, shrimp, green onions and cilantro. Simmer for 2 to 3 minutes.
5. Increase heat to high and add the bean sprouts and chicken-shrimp mixture. Toss well.
6. Serve immediately with crushed peanuts, additional soy sauce and hot sauce.

Serves 4

Pierogies with Potato Vodka Butter

Now this is food to warm your soul—couch food at its best. You get one hour of nap time after this meal.

4 1/2 cups all-purpose flour

12 tbsp. butter

4 tsp. salt

2 large eggs, lightly beaten

2 tbsp. vegetable oil

1/2 to 1 cup water

3 large onions

4 large russet potatoes, peeled and quartered

1 1/2 cups cubed Velveeta cheese

1 tsp. chopped fresh thyme

1 tsp. Bone Dust BBQ Spice (see page 42)

1 tsp. white pepper

8 slices thick-cut bacon, diced

1 oz. potato vodka

2 tbsp. chopped fresh parsley

1 cup sour cream

1. In a stand mixer fitted with the dough hook, combine the flour, 7 tbsp. of the butter and 2 tsp. of the salt. Mix on low speed until well blended. Add the eggs, oil and 1/2 cup of the water. Mix on low speed for 8 to 10 minutes or until the dough is smooth but not sticky. If necessary, add a little more water to get a smooth dough. Form the dough into a ball and wrap in plastic. Let rest for at least 30 minutes.
2. Meanwhile, mince 1 onion; set aside. Slice remaining 2 onions; set aside.
3. Cook the potatoes in a large pot of boiling salted water until tender. Drain well and return to heat to dry for 30 seconds while shaking the pan. Mash the potatoes. Place in a large bowl.
4. In a large frying pan over medium-high heat, melt 2 tbsp. of the butter. Fry the minced onion, stirring, for 5 to 8 minutes, until tender but not browned. Add to the potatoes. Set the pan aside.
5. To the potatoes, add the Velveeta cheese, thyme, Bone Dust BBQ Spice, the remaining 2 tsp. salt and the pepper. Gently fold until cheese is melted and everything is well mixed.

6. On a lightly floured surface, roll out the dough until 1/8 inch thick. Using a 4-inch pastry cutter or a glass, cut out circles. Place 1 1/2 tbsp. of filling in the centre of each disc. Wet the edges with a little water and fold in half to make a half moon, pressing lightly around the filling to force out extra air. Crimp edges with a fork to seal.

7. In the frying pan over medium heat, cook the bacon until it is lightly crisp. Add the sliced onions and cook, stirring frequently, 8 to 10 minutes or until golden brown. Transfer bacon and onions to a bowl.

8. Bring a large pot of salted water to a rolling boil. Add pierogies and cook for 5 to 7 minutes, until pierogies float and are tender. Drain well.

9. Working quickly, melt the remaining 3 tbsp. butter in the frying pan. Fry the cooked pierogies for 3 to 5 minutes per side, until golden brown and lightly crisp. Add the vodka and cook for about 1 minute, stirring to scrape up any brown bits. Stir in the bacon mixture and parsley.

10. Transfer to a big bowl and serve immediately, garnished with dollops of sour cream.

Serves 4

Note: You can also make the dough in a food processor fitted with the dough blade. Pulse the ingredients until a smooth dough forms.

Planked Polenta on the Board
with Grill-Roasted Mushrooms and Goat Cheese

My friend Wendy introduced me to Valerie Mitchell, author of a great Italian family cookbook called *Polenta on the Board*. Here's my version of her classic family recipe, done on a cedar plank.

1 large Portobello mushroom cap

6 large white mushrooms

3 large oyster mushrooms

3 large shiitake mushroom caps

2 cups hot water

1/4 cup balsamic vinegar

1/4 cup olive oil

1 tbsp. Bone Dust BBQ Spice (see page 42)

1 large sweet onion, cut into 1/2-inch rings

1 cup crumbled goat cheese

1 tbsp. chopped fresh basil

Salt and pepper

2 cups Really Good Roasted Chicken Stock (see page 71)

1 tsp. salt

1 cup cornmeal

2 tbsp. butter

1/2 cup grated Asiago cheese

Special equipment: 1 untreated cedar plank (at least 10 × 12 inches and 1/2 inch thick),
   soaked in cold water for at least 1 hour

1. Preheat grill to medium-high.
2. Place the mushrooms in a large bowl. Add the hot water. Place a plate on top of the mushrooms to help keep them submerged. Let mushrooms soak for 15 minutes. (This will keep them from drying out on the grill.) Drain mushrooms and return to the bowl. Add the vinegar, oil and Bone Dust BBQ Spice. Toss to coat.
3. Grill mushrooms (reserving vinegar mixture), turning once, for 8 to 12 minutes or until tender and lightly charred.

4. Meanwhile, brush onion rings with the vinegar mixture and grill onions for 8 to 10 minutes, turning once, until lightly charred and tender.

5. Let mushrooms and onions cool slightly, then cut into 1-inch chunks. In a bowl combine mushrooms, onions, goat cheese and basil. Season to taste with salt, pepper and a dash or two of balsamic vinegar and olive oil. Set aside.

6. In a large saucepan, bring the Really Good Roasted Chicken Stock to a boil over high heat. Add 1 tsp. salt. Reduce heat to medium-low and add cornmeal in a steady stream while whisking constantly. Using a wooden spoon, stir constantly for 15 to 20 minutes, until cornmeal is thick and smooth. Remove from heat.

7. Stir in the butter and 1/4 cup of the Asiago cheese until smooth. Season polenta with salt and pepper to taste. Let cool in the pot about 5 minutes.

8. Preheat grill to high.

9. Spoon cooling polenta onto the cedar plank, piling it high and leaving a 1-inch border around the edge of the plank. Make a little well in the centre of the polenta and fill with the mushroom mixture. Sprinkle with remaining Asiago cheese.

10. Place plank on the centre of the grill and close the lid. Bake for 10 to 15 minutes or until the polenta is lightly browned and hot. (If the plank should ignite, reduce the heat and douse the flames with a spray bottle of water.)

11. Set the plank on a heat-proof platter. Place in the centre of the table and have everyone serve themselves.

Serves 4 to 6

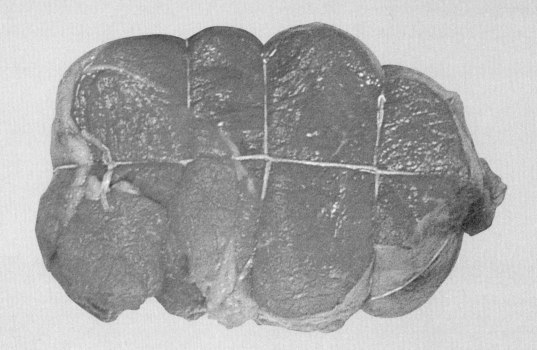

For the love of meat

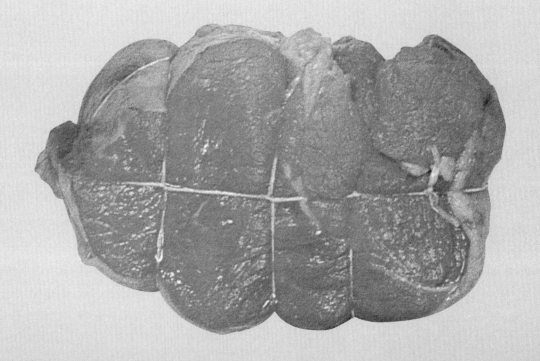

Yukon Jack Beef Ribs with Gold Rush Honey Garlic Sauce

This recipe appeared in the *Better Homes and Gardens* grilling issue in 2003. What makes it so great is the Yukon Jack rye liqueur. The low-and-slow cooking makes the meat fall cleanly from the bone.

2 racks beef ribs (each about 3 lb.)

2 tbsp. Bone Dust BBQ Spice (see page 42)

2 lemons, sliced

1/2 cup Yukon Jack liqueur

1 can ginger ale

Gold Rush Honey Garlic Sauce

2 tbsp. vegetable oil

6 cloves garlic, minced

1 jalapeño pepper, seeded and finely chopped

1/4 cup diced onion

2 cups honey

1 cup Really Good Roasted Chicken Stock (see page 71)

1/2 cup rice vinegar

1/4 cup Yukon Jack liqueur

3 tbsp. prepared mustard

2 tsp. dry mustard

1 tsp. black mustard seeds

2 tsp. cornstarch

3 tbsp. cold water

1 tsp. black pepper

1/2 tsp. cayenne pepper

Salt to taste

1. Preheat oven to 325°F.
2. Using a sharp knife, score the membrane on the backside of the ribs in a diamond pattern. Rub with the Bone Dust BBQ Spice, pressing the spices into the meat. Lay the ribs, meat side down, in a roasting pan. Lay three or four slices of lemon on each rib. Pour in the Yukon Jack liqueur and ginger ale. Cover tightly with lid or foil. Braise ribs until tender, 2 to 2 1/2 hours. Let cool slightly. Remove ribs from braising liquid.
3. While the ribs are cooking, prepare the sauce. In a medium saucepan over medium-high heat, heat the oil. Sauté the garlic, jalapeño pepper and onion for 2 to 3 minutes, until onion is tender. Stir in the honey, chicken stock, rice vinegar, Yukon Jack liqueur, prepared mustard, dry mustard and mustard seeds. Bring to a boil, reduce heat to low and simmer for 10 minutes, stirring occasionally.
4. Combine the cornstarch and water; stir the mixture into the sauce and return to a boil. Boil, stirring, for 1 to 2 minutes, until the sauce thickens. Stir in black pepper, cayenne and salt. Let cool.
5. Preheat grill to medium-high. Grill ribs, basting with the Gold Rush Honey Garlic Sauce, for 8 to 10 minutes per side or until lightly charred and fully cooked. Cut between every third rib and serve.

Serves 4 to 6

Pan-Fried Tenderloin Steaks with Whipped Cognac Marrow Butter

This dish was prepared by my friend Olaf, for my wife, Pamela, and me at our first wedding anniversary bash. It's a rich and succulent dish that, I swear, brings you one step closer to heaven.

8 beef tenderloin medallions (each 4 oz. and 1 inch thick)

6 large veal marrow bones

1/4 cup butter, softened

2 tsp. chopped fresh thyme

Sea salt and pepper to taste

1/4 cup Garlic Herb Steak Paste (see page 47)

2 tbsp. olive oil

2 tbsp. cognac

1. Using a small spoon, scoop the marrow from the centre of the bones. (You will need 1/2 to 3/4 cup of marrow.) In a food processor, combine marrow and the butter. Blend until smooth, scraping down the sides of the bowl if necessary. Add the thyme, salt and pepper. Process until blended. Transfer marrow butter to a serving bowl and set aside.
2. Rub the Garlic Herb Steak Paste into the beef. In a large, heavy frying pan over medium-high heat, heat the oil. Sauté the beef for 1 to 2 minutes or until lightly browned on the bottom. Turn beef and sauté for 1 to 2 minutes longer for medium-rare. Remove from heat.
3. Slowly add cognac to the pan and light with a kitchen match. Be careful of the flame. Flambé until the flames die down.
4. Stir in 2 tbsp. of the marrow butter. Transfer medallions to plates and drizzle with Cognac Marrow Butter. Top each steak with a dollop of reserved marrow butter.

Serves 4

Roast Prime Rib with Green Peppercorn Gravy

The best prime rib I've ever had was at the Chicago Chop House Restaurant, ranked as one of the top 10 best steak houses in the U.S.A. Their prime rib was so good I woke up in the middle of the night dreaming of this great meat. On a drooling scale of 1 to 10, this prime rib ranks 100.

8 cloves garlic, minced

1/4 cup Amazing Steak Spice (see page 43)

1 prime rib roast (5 to 6 lb., with at least 4 ribs)

4 sprigs fresh rosemary or thyme

Green Peppercorn Gravy

2 tbsp. butter, softened

2 tbsp. all-purpose flour

1 1/2 cups Really Good Beef Stock (see page 70)

2 tbsp. brandy

2 tbsp. green peppercorns in brine, drained

Salt and pepper

Prepared horseradish

1. Preheat oven to 425°F.
2. In a bowl, combine the garlic and Amazing Steak Spice. Rub all over the prime rib, pressing the spices into the meat so they adhere. Place prime rib on a rack in a roasting pan. Cover with rosemary or thyme sprigs. Roast, uncovered, for 20 minutes. Reduce heat to 325°F and roast for 15 to 18 minutes per pound for rare (a meat thermometer will read 140°F), 20 to 25 minutes per pound for medium (165°F) or 25 to 30 minutes per pound for well done (180°F), g-d forbid.
3. Transfer prime rib to a carving board and let rest for about 10 minutes.
4. Meanwhile, prepare the Green Peppercorn Gravy. In a small bowl, mash together the butter and flour; set aside. Skim fat from pan juices and transfer the juices to a medium saucepan. Add the beef stock and brandy. Bring to a low boil over medium heat. Whisk in the butter and flour paste, 1 tbsp. at a time, whisking until smooth and thick. Add green peppercorns, and salt and pepper to taste. Remove from heat and keep warm.
5. Carve the prime rib between every bone into four large chops. Serve drizzled with the gravy, with horseradish on the side.

Serves 4

Big Man's Porterhouse Steak #3 with Guinness Syrup

My steak. My way. (It's a hefty one but well worth it.) One steak should serve one but can serve up to four.

1 porterhouse steak (2 lb. and 2 to 3 inches thick)

2 cans Guinness

1/4 cup maple syrup

1 tbsp. Dijon mustard

2 tbsp. cold butter, cut into pieces

2 tbsp. chopped fresh herbs (such as rosemary, thyme, parsley)

Salt and pepper

4 cloves garlic, minced

2 tbsp. olive oil

1 tbsp. Amazing Steak Spice (see page 43)

1. Place the steak in a glass dish about 3 inches deep. Pour in 1 can of the Guinness. Marinate, covered and refrigerated, for 4 to 6 hours or overnight, turning occasionally.

2. Pour the remaining can of Guinness into a small saucepan. Bring to a boil over high heat. Reduce heat to medium and simmer for 10 to 15 minutes, until the beer reduces by three quarters. Stir in the maple syrup and mustard. Remove from heat. Stir in the butter a little at a time, stirring until incorporated. Stir in the herbs, and salt and pepper to taste. Set Guinness Syrup aside, keeping warm.

3. Preheat broiler.

4. In a bowl, combine the garlic, oil and Amazing Steak Spice. Remove steak from marinade, discarding the marinade. Rub the steak with the steak spice mixture, pressing the spices into the meat.

5. Place the steak in a broiler pan. With the oven door open slightly, broil the steak 2 or 3 inches below the heat until browned, 3 to 5 minutes. Close the door, reduce heat to 425°F and roast steak, basting with Guinness Syrup, for 30 to 40 minutes for rare or 40 to 60 minutes for medium-rare.

6. Serve with Lobster and Brie Mashed Potatoes (see page 212).

Serves 1 to 4

Best Damn Pepper Steak

For best results, use a heavy-bottomed frying pan. I prefer to use a cast-iron pan: it holds the heat and cooks the steak evenly. I still remember my first peppercorn steak, prepared for me by my grandfather, Opi, whose secret was using only the freshest of black pepper. He would crack the peppercorns under his cast-iron pan.

1 tbsp. kosher salt

1/4 cup coarsely ground black pepper

4 centre-cut New York strip steaks (each 8 to 12 oz. and 1 1/2 inches thick)

Horseradish Butter Sauce

1/4 cup butter

1/4 cup chopped shallots

2 tbsp. cognac

2 cloves garlic, minced

2 tbsp. chopped fresh herbs (such as rosemary, thyme, parsley)

1 tbsp. prepared horseradish

1 tbsp. balsamic vinegar

Salt and pepper

1. In a small bowl, stir together the salt and pepper. Season the steaks with salt and pepper mixture, pressing the spices into the meat so they adhere.
2. In a well-ventilated kitchen, heat a large, heavy frying pan over high heat until the pan begins to lightly smoke. Cook steaks until browned on one side, 2 to 4 minutes. Turn steaks and continue cooking until desired doneness (2 to 4 minutes for rare to medium-rare). Reduce heat to low. Transfer steaks to a platter and cover loosely with foil to keep warm.
3. Return the pan to the stove and melt the butter. Add the shallots and cook, stirring, for 1 minute. Add the cognac, stirring to scrape up any brown bits from the bottom of the pan. Add the herbs, horseradish and garlic, stirring until heated. Stir in the balsamic vinegar and season to taste with salt and pepper. Remove from heat.
4. Cut the steaks diagonally into 1/2-inch-thick slices. Serve drizzled with the Horseradish Butter Sauce.

Serves 4

Shot and Beer Oven-Q'ed Pot Roast

A well-cooked pot roast should be tender and should easily fall apart. My mom's used to be so tender that she carved it with a fork. I would toss the leftover shredded pot roast with raw onions and drizzle it with BBQ sauce. Served on a dinner roll, this was a comfort meal for me.

3 tbsp. all-purpose flour

2 tbsp. Bone Dust BBQ Spice (see page 42)

1 beef chuck pot roast (4 to 5 lb.)

3 tbsp. vegetable shortening

2 large sweet onions, sliced

8 cloves garlic, minced

2 red chilies, minced

1 cup Really Good Tomato Sauce (see page 73)

1/2 cup ketchup

1/2 cup Jack Daniel's

1/4 cup brown sugar

1/4 cup malt vinegar

2 tbsp. Dijon mustard

1/2 bottle lager

Salt and pepper

2 tbsp. chopped fresh cilantro

1 lime, cut into wedges

1. Preheat oven to 325°F.
2. In a bowl, combine the flour and Bone Dust BBQ Spice. Evenly coat the pot roast with the seasoned flour.
3. Melt the shortening in a large, heavy frying pan over medium-high heat. Sear meat on all sides. Transfer meat to a large roasting pan.
4. Add onions, garlic and chilies to the frying pan; sauté for 10 to 15 minutes, until onions are browned. Add the tomato sauce, ketchup, Jack Daniel's, brown sugar, vinegar, mustard and beer. Season to taste with salt and pepper. Bring to a boil, stirring. Pour over the pot roast. Cover and cook for 3 to 3 1/2 hours or until meat is tender.
5. Remove pot roast from the pan and skim the fat. Stir the pan sauce. Slice or shred the roast and ladle the pan sauce over it. Serve garnished with cilantro and lime wedges. Serve with mashed potatoes.

Serves 8

Oven-Smoked Brisket o' Beef

Low and slow is the key to making this brisket perfect. The aroma of smoke and meat in your home will be intoxicating. I like to buy a fat brisket, but you can get 'em how you like 'em.

1 beef brisket (3 to 4 lb.)

1/4 cup Amazing Steak Spice (see page 43)

3 large onions, cut into 1-inch pieces

3 tbsp. butter, cut in pieces

1/2 cup your favourite BBQ sauce

Special equipment: 1 untreated cedar plank (at least 8 × 10 inches and 1 inch thick), soaked in cold water for at least 1 hour

1. Preheat oven to 325°F.
2. Place the plank in a large roasting pan. Heat plank in oven for 5 to 10 minutes or until you begin to smell the sweet scent of cedar.
3. Rub the brisket liberally with the Amazing Steak Spice, pressing the spices into the meat.
4. Spread half of the onions evenly over the plank. Lay the brisket over the onions. Top with remaining onions, spreading evenly. Cover tightly with foil and roast for 60 to 75 minutes per pound or until tender.
5. Scrape the onions off the brisket and transfer brisket to a serving platter. Cover loosely with foil to keep warm. Remove plank from roasting pan. Stir onions on the plank. Stir in the butter a little at a time, stirring until melted. Stir in the BBQ sauce.
6. Slice brisket across the grain and serve topped with a spoonful of smoky BBQ onions.

Serves 8

Ginger Beef Stir-Fry with Broccoli and Almonds

Here's a quick-and-easy stir-fry for those times when you want dinner in a hurry.

1 beef tenderloin (8 oz.)

1/4 cup tapioca starch

1/4 cup peanut oil

1 small onion, cut into 1-inch pieces

1 stalk celery, thinly sliced diagonally

8 spears asparagus, cut into 2-inch pieces

2 cups 1/2-inch broccoli florets

1 tbsp. minced fresh ginger

1/4 cup Chinese rice wine

1/2 tsp. coarsely ground black pepper

1/4 cup oyster sauce

1 tbsp. soy sauce

1 tbsp. rice vinegar

1 tsp. toasted sesame seeds

1/4 cup smokehouse-flavoured almonds

2 green onions, thinly sliced diagonally

1. Freeze the tenderloin for 30 minutes (this makes it easier to slice). Slice the tenderloin in half lengthwise, then cut each half into 1/4-inch slices. Toss the beef with the tapioca starch to coat.

2. Heat the oil over high heat in a wok or deep frying pan. Quickly sear the beef, stirring, about 1 1/2 minutes. Remove from pan and set aside.

3. Add onion and celery to wok. Stir-fry for 30 seconds to 1 minute, until lightly browned and tender. Add asparagus, broccoli and ginger. Stir-fry for 1 to 2 minutes, until lightly seared. Stir in the wine and pepper; cover and bring to a boil.

4. Add oyster sauce, soy sauce, vinegar and sesame seeds. Toss to coat. Stir in beef and bring to a boil. Stir in almonds and green onions.

5. Serve immediately over steamed rice.

Serves 2

Kick-Ass Tailgating Chili

Seven friends and I loaded up the truck one afternoon and headed to Buffalo to see the Buffalo Bills play Detroit. Tailgating was at the top of the list of things to do. Second was beer, and last was football. We had a blast, and this big pot of chili was a crowd-pleaser. At one time there were about 20 football fans around our truck having a taste of chili. It's all beef and no beans.

2 lb. regular ground beef

1 lb. ground pork

1 lb. steak (flank, round, blade, skirt or sirloin), cut into
  1/2-inch cubes

1/4 cup Bone Dust BBQ Spice (see page 42)

2 tbsp. salt

2 tbsp. Mexican chili powder

2 tbsp. ground cumin

1 tbsp. cayenne pepper

1 tbsp. dry mustard

1 tbsp. dried oregano

1/2 lb. bacon, diced

6 cloves garlic, minced

3 medium onions, diced

3 jalapeño peppers, seeded and diced

1/2 cup vegetable oil

1 bottle lager

2 cups Really Good Beef Stock (see page 70)

2 cups K of the Q Beer BBQ Sauce or other gourmet BBQ sauce

2 cups shredded Cheddar cheese

1 cup sour cream

8 slices Texas toast

1. In a large bowl, combine the ground beef, ground pork and cubed steak. In a small bowl, combine the Bone Dust BBQ Spice, salt, chili powder, cumin, cayenne, mustard and oregano. Pour the spices over the meats and mix thoroughly until meat is well coated. Marinate, covered and refrigerated, for 1 hour.

2. In a large frying pan, sauté the bacon until it is just starting to crisp, 3 to 5 minutes. Add the garlic, onions and jalapeño peppers. Sauté for 3 to 5 more minutes, until the onions are tender. Strain the onion mixture, reserving the fat. Transfer the onion mixture to a large soup pot.

3. In the same frying pan, heat the reserved fat and 2 tbsp. of the vegetable oil over medium-high heat. Working in batches, sauté the seasoned meat until the meat is fully cooked, adding extra oil as necessary. Using a slotted spoon, transfer the meat as cooked to the soup pot.

4. Add the beer and stock to the meat; bring to a low boil, stirring constantly. Reduce heat to low and simmer, stirring occasionally, for 1 hour. Stir in the BBQ sauce and remove from heat.

5. Ladle into bowls and garnish with shredded cheese and sour cream. Serve with the Texas toast.

Serves 8

Holy $!*%, There's a Block of Cheese in My Meat Loaf

"Okay, now you're getting ridiculous!" That's what my wife, Pamela, said after I pulled this meat loaf out of the oven. It's loaded with cheese—a whole three-quarter-pound block. All you really need to know is, when you're done eating, dial 911 and ask for cardiac care. Even better, if you can move, go for a jog. A really long jog. Or just roll over to the couch.

1 block (12 oz./350 g) Monterey Jack cheese, cut in half lengthwise

1 lb. ground pork

2 lb. regular ground beef

1 medium onion, diced

4 cloves garlic, finely chopped

3 tbsp. Dijon mustard

2 tbsp. Bone Dust BBQ Spice (see page 42)

1 tbsp. salt

1 tbsp. dry mustard

1 tbsp. Worcestershire sauce

2 tsp. cayenne pepper

2 tsp. black pepper

1 tsp. garlic salt

1 tsp. ground cumin

1 tsp. chili powder

3 slices bacon

1/2 cup BBQ sauce

1. Freeze the cheese until solid, about 1 1/2 hours.
2. In a bowl, combine the ground pork and ground beef. Add the onion, garlic, mustard, Bone Dust BBQ Spice, salt, mustard, Worcestershire sauce, cayenne, black pepper, garlic salt, cumin and chili powder. With your hands, mix thoroughly until all the seasonings are well distributed through the meat, about 3 minutes.
3. Line the bottom of a 9 × 5-inch meat loaf pan with the bacon. Pour two thirds of the meat mixture into the pan, packing it firmly to press out excess air. Press the two pieces of frozen cheese into the meat mixture, leaving a 1-inch meat border around the edges of the cheese. Top with the remaining meat and press to form a tight seal between the meat layers. Cover and refrigerate for 1 hour to let the meat relax.
4. Preheat oven to 375°F.
5. Place the pan on a baking sheet. Baste the meat loaf with some of the BBQ sauce. Bake on middle rack of oven, basting with BBQ sauce every 15 minutes, until the meat loaf is fully cooked (a meat thermometer in the meat—not the cheese—will read 180°F) and the cheese is soft.
6. Drain excess fat from meat loaf. Invert meat loaf onto a platter and remove the pan. Cut into 6 to 8 thick slices and serve. Cheers, and be sure to have a beer with this.

Serves 6 to 8

Stuff

My mom's creation! Whenever she made this beef dish, my brothers and I would say, "What is it?" and Mom would reply, "It's Stuff!" That's all we knew until one day I watched and learned that stuff is … well, stuff!

1 lb. regular ground beef

1 tbsp. Bone Dust BBQ Spice (see page 42)

6 tbsp. butter

3 cloves garlic, minced

1 medium onion, diced

1 tbsp. Dijon mustard

1 tsp. Worcestershire sauce

1/2 cup heavy cream

Salt and pepper

1. In a bowl, mix together the ground beef and Bone Dust BBQ Spice.
2. In a large frying pan over medium-high heat, melt 3 tbsp. of the butter. Sauté the ground beef, in batches, until fully cooked and lightly browned. Drain the beef in a colander.
3. Melt 1 tbsp. of the butter in the pan. Sauté the garlic and onion for 3 to 5 minutes, until lightly browned and tender. Return beef to the pan and cook, stirring, for 2 to 3 minutes or until heated through. Stir in the mustard and Worcestershire sauce. Bring to a boil, stirring to ensure that nothing sticks to the bottom of the pan. Stir in the cream. Return to a boil, stirring. Reduce heat to low and simmer, stirring frequently, until thick and creamy, 5 to 10 minutes.
4. Serve hot, spooned over mashed potatoes.

Serves 4 to 6

Porto-Braised Oxtail

This is a super Sunday meal for those cold winter weekends. Use oxtail pieces cut from the thick end of the tail. It's easier to eat and has more meat.

3 lb. oxtails (2-inch-thick pieces)

1 bottle (750 mL) port

1 cup all-purpose flour

1 tbsp. Bone Dust BBQ Spice (see page 42)

1 tbsp. ground black pepper

2 tsp. salt

3 tbsp. olive oil

6 cloves garlic, minced

1 medium onion, finely diced

1 stalk celery, finely diced

1 medium carrot, finely diced

1 small butternut squash, cut into 1-inch cubes

2 cups peeled pearl onions

1 bay leaf

2 sprigs fresh thyme

6 peppercorns

3 cups Really Good Beef Stock (see page 70) or demi-glace would be even better

2 tbsp. cold butter, cut in pieces

1. Place the oxtails in a baking dish large enough to hold them in one layer. Cover with the port. Marinate, covered and refrigerated, for 4 to 6 hours.
2. Remove oxtails from port and set aside. Pour port into a saucepan and bring to a boil. Reduce heat and simmer for 30 minutes or until reduced by half.
3. Preheat oven to 325° F.
4. In a large bowl, stir together the flour, Bone Dust BBQ Spice, pepper and salt. Dredge oxtails in the seasoned flour.
5. In a large frying pan, heat the oil over high heat. Sear the oxtails on all sides, in batches if necessary, about 5 minutes. Transfer to a roasting pan.

6.	In the same pan, heat 2 tbsp. of the oil over medium-high heat. Sauté the garlic, onion, celery and carrot for 4 to 6 minutes or until tender. Add the squash and pearl onions; cook, stirring occasionally, for 5 minutes. Pour vegetables over the oxtails. Add the bay leaf, thyme and peppercorns; shake the pan to even things out slightly. Pour in the reduced port and the stock. Cover and bake, checking the liquid periodically and adding more stock or water if needed, for 3 hours or until the oxtail is fully cooked and can easily be pulled from the bone. Transfer oxtails to a platter and keep warm.

7.	Discard the bay leaf. Skim excess fat from pan juices. Bring to a boil. Stir in cold butter until incorporated. Remove from heat.

8.	Spoon sauce, onions and squash over the oxtails. If you wish you can remove the meat from the bone for easier eating. Serve with Planked Polenta on the Board (see page 126).

Serves 6

Tip:	To make peeling the onions easier, soak them in warm water for 10 minutes to moisten the skin and loosen it from the onion.

Chinese-Style Honey Garlic Spareribs

More real Canadian Chinese food. You always eat too much. "You go home now" is what the guy at the Chinese food buffet likes to say to me.

2 racks pork spareribs (each about 3 lb.)
3 cups Really Good Chicken Stock (see page 71)
    or pineapple juice
6 cloves garlic, minced
2 whole star anise
1 cinnamon stick
1/4 cup soy sauce
2 tbsp. sugar
2 tbsp. salt
1 tsp. peppercorns
2 tsp. sesame seeds
2 tsp. thinly sliced green onion

Honey Garlic Sauce
6 cloves garlic, minced
1/4 cup brown sugar
1/4 cup honey
1/4 cup soy sauce
1 cup Really Good Chicken Stock (see page 71)
Salt and pepper

1. Have your butcher cut the racks of spareribs lengthwise into 3 long strips 1 to 2 inches wide. Cut between every bone and set aside.
2. In a large saucepan, combine the stock, garlic, star anise, cinnamon, soy sauce, sugar, salt and peppercorns; stir to dissolve the salt and sugar. Bring to a rolling boil. Add spareribs a few at a time. Return to the boil. Reduce heat and simmer, uncovered and stirring occasionally, until pork is tender, about 1 1/2 hours. Drain.
3. Preheat oven to 350°F.
4. To make the sauce, in a large bowl, stir together the garlic, brown sugar, honey, soy sauce, stock, and salt and pepper to taste. Add the ribs and turn to coat. Spread coated ribs evenly in a deep roasting pan. Roast, uncovered, for 15 to 20 minutes, until hot, sticky and crispy.
5. Transfer ribs to a serving bowl. Garnish with sesame seeds and green onions. Serve with fried rice.

Serves 6 to 8

Honeydew Pork Ribs

When I was a kid, it was a real treat to be able to go to the Canadian National Exhibition. The Flyer and Jumbo Jet roller coasters and the Alpine Way Tram were a must. And then there was the Food Building, with more varieties of food than you could imagine. The first thing I did was head to the Honeydew booth for an ice-cold glass of a sweet honey-flavoured orange drink. Frozen Honeydew concentrate can be a little hard to find. Substitute frozen concentrated orange juice if you can't find the honeydew concentrate.

1 can (12 oz./341 mL) Honeydew Orange Concentrate
  or frozen orange juice concentrate
1 large onion, sliced
1/2 cup thinly sliced peeled fresh ginger
4 racks pork baby back ribs (each 1 to 1 1/2 lb.)
1/4 cup Bone Dust BBQ Spice (see page 42)
2 oranges, each cut into 8 slices
1 cup water

Honeydew Glazing Sauce
1/2 cup honey
2 tbsp. rice vinegar
1 tsp. hot dry mustard
1 tsp. sambal oelek
Salt and pepper
1 tbsp. chopped fresh cilantro

1. Preheat oven to 325°F.
2. Prepare Honeydew juice according to the package instructions; set aside.
3. Spread the onions and ginger evenly in the bottom of a roasting pan. Using a sharp knife, score the skin side of the ribs in a diamond pattern. Rub with the Bone Dust BBQ Spice, pressing the seasoning into the meat so it adheres. Lay the ribs, meat side down and overlapping slightly, on top of the onion and ginger mixture. Lay 4 slices of orange over each rack of ribs. Pour in the water and 1 cup of the Honeydew juice. Cover.
4. Braise for 2 to 2 1/2 hours, until the ribs are tender. To test for doneness, pull on a rib bone; it should easily pull from the meat. Discard the orange slices and carefully transfer the ribs, meat side up, to a baking sheet; set aside.
5. Preheat oven to 425°F.
6. To prepare the glazing sauce, in a blender or food processor, purée 1 cup of the braised onion and ginger mixture. Add the honey, vinegar, mustard, sambal oelek and 1 more cup of Honeydew juice. Blend until smooth. Transfer to a saucepan and bring to a low boil over medium heat. Season to taste with salt and pepper. Remove from heat and stir in the cilantro.
7. Baste ribs with some of the Honeydew Glazing Sauce. Roast the ribs, basting occasionally, until hot and sticky, 10 to 12 minutes. Slice between every third rib and serve.

Serves 4 to 8

Cranberry Pork Tenderloin

Marinating the pork in the cranberry juice tenderizes it and adds flavour. Be sure not to overcook the pork—it's quite lean and dries out if overcooked.

2 cups pure cranberry juice

2 to 3 tbsp. Garlic Herb Steak Paste (see page 47)

2 tsp. salt

2 pork tenderloins (each 1 to 1 1/2 lb.), trimmed of silverskin

Salt and pepper

2 tbsp. oil

1 tbsp. butter

2 medium shallots, thinly sliced

1/2 cup orange juice

1 tsp. orange zest

1 tbsp. chopped fresh sage

1 tsp. coarsely ground black pepper

1 cup dried cranberries

1/2 cup diced peeled green apple

1/2 cup honey

1. In a glass dish large enough to hold the tenderloins in one layer, stir together the cranberry juice, Garlic Herb Steak Paste and salt. Add the pork and turn to coat. Marinate, covered and refrigerated, for 4 to 6 hours or overnight.

2. Preheat oven to 425°F.

3. Remove pork from marinade, discarding marinade. Pat pork dry with paper towels. Season to taste with salt and pepper.

4. Heat the oil in a large oven-proof frying pan over medium-high heat. Sear the pork on all sides. Transfer pan to the oven and roast pork for 10 to 12 minutes for medium-rare. Let rest for a few minutes before slicing.

5. Meanwhile, in a small saucepan over medium-high heat, melt the butter. Sauté the shallots until tender, 30 seconds to 1 minute. Add orange juice, orange zest, sage and pepper. Bring to a boil, stirring. Add the cranberries, apple and honey. Return to a boil, stirring. Reduce heat to low and simmer, stirring, for 10 to 15 minutes or until cranberries are soft and the sauce has thickened. Set aside, keeping warm.

6. Cut the pork into 1/2-inch-thick slices. Serve topped with the cranberry apple sauce. Serve with Wendy's Creamed Peas (see page 214).

Serves 4

Beer'n'Brats with Honey Beer Mustard

While on a 40th-birthday golf trip in Hilton Head with my longtime buddies Chris, Cal and Eddy, I made this meal for one of our after-golf poker nights.

Honey Beer Mustard

1/4 cup honey

3 tbsp. hot dry mustard

3 tbsp. Pilsner beer

1 tbsp. grainy Dijon mustard

8 bratwurst

1 lb. canned or jarred sauerkraut

1/4 tsp. caraway seeds

1/4 tsp. mustard seeds

2 cups Pilsner beer

8 slices thick-cut bacon

8 poppyseed egg buns or sausage buns, halved and toasted

1. To prepare the Honey Beer Mustard, in a bowl, combine the honey, dry mustard, beer and grainy mustard. Stir until smooth. Set aside.
2. Preheat oven to 375°F.
3. Place the bratwurst in a roasting pan. In a bowl, stir together the sauerkraut, caraway seeds and mustard seeds. Spread evenly over the brats. Pour in the beer. Layer bacon over top. Bake, uncovered, for 1 hour.
4. Coarsely chop the bacon. Drain beer from the pan. Place brats in toasted buns, top with sauerkraut and garnish with Honey Beer Mustard. Sprinkle with the bacon. Serve with beer!

Serves 4 hungry dudes or dudettes

Roast Rack of Pork with Vanilla Coke BBQ Sauce

As a kid, having a soda fountain vanilla Coke was always a special treat. When Coca-Cola introduced the Vanilla Coke a few years ago, it brought back a flood of childhood memories. For me, this isn't an everyday drink (I prefer the original Coke), but it is the ingredient that makes this barbecue sauce rock.

1 frenched rack of pork (3 to 4 lb., with 6 or 7 bones)

2 cups water

1/4 cup salt

1 can Vanilla Coke

2 tbsp. Bone Dust BBQ Spice (see page 42)

2 medium onions, cut into 8 wedges

4 medium carrots, cut into 2-inch-long sticks

4 medium parsnips, cut into 2-inch-long sticks

Vanilla Coke BBQ Sauce

2 tbsp. butter

6 cloves garlic, minced

1 small onion, finely diced

2 tsp. minced fresh ginger

1 tsp. Bone Dust BBQ Spice (see page 42)

1/2 cup packed brown sugar

1 can Vanilla Coke

1 cup Really Good Roasted Chicken Stock (see page 71)

2 tbsp. soy sauce

2 tbsp. rice vinegar

2 tsp. tapioca starch or cornstarch

1 tbsp. water

2 tsp. toasted sesame seeds

Salt and pepper

1. Place the pork in a roasting pan. In a bowl, stir together the water, salt and Vanilla Coke. Pour over the pork. Marinate, covered and refrigerated, for 24 hours.

2. Preheat oven to 425°F.

3. Remove pork from marinade, discarding marinade. Rinse pork under cold running water and pat dry with paper towels. Rub with 2 tbsp. of the Bone Dust BBQ Spice, pressing the spices into the meat. Place pork on a rack in the roasting pan. Scatter the onions, carrots and parsnips around the pork. Roast for 30 minutes.

4. Meanwhile, prepare the Vanilla Coke BBQ Sauce. In a medium saucepan over medium-high heat, melt the butter. Sauté the garlic, onion and ginger for 3 to 5 minutes, until onion is tender. Stir in the Bone Dust BBQ Spice. Add the brown sugar and stir until blended. Stir in the Vanilla Coke, stock, soy sauce and rice vinegar. Bring to a low boil, stirring occasionally. Stir the tapioca starch into the water; stir

into the sauce. Return to the boil, reduce heat and simmer until sauce thickens. Remove from heat and stir in sesame seeds, and salt and pepper to taste.

5. Reduce oven temperature to 350°F and baste pork with some of the sauce. Roast, basting occasionally, for 15 to 20 minutes per pound (45 to 60 minutes for medium); a meat thermometer should read between 145 and 150°F. Let roast rest for 10 minutes before carving.

6. Carve roast into 1/2-inch-thick slices. Serve with the pan-roasted vegetables and remaining Vanilla Coke BBQ Sauce for dipping.

Serves 6

Oven-Roasted Rack of Lamb Crusted with Dijon, Goat Cheese and Macadamia Nuts (page 151)

Butterflied Quail with Hoisin Honey BBQ Baste (page 178)

Mike's Mom's Pork Chop and Scalloped Potato Bake

This is Chef Mike's Mama Bonnie's family recipe for a one-pot meal. Pork chops, potatoes, cream and cheese. Ahhhhhhhh!

8 bone-in pork rib chops (each 6 oz. and 1 inch thick)

3 tbsp. Bone Dust BBQ Spice (see page 42)

3 tbsp. vegetable oil

1 lb. white mushrooms, thinly sliced

1 large Portobello mushroom, gills removed, thinly sliced

1 large Vidalia onion, thinly sliced

4 cloves garlic, minced

Salt and pepper

8 to 10 unpeeled Yukon Gold potatoes, thinly sliced

1 cup grated Parmesan cheese

2 tbsp. chopped fresh herbs (such as sage, rosemary, thyme and parsley)

2 cups heavy cream

2 cups Really Good Roasted Chicken Stock (see page 71)

1. Season the chops with the Bone Dust BBQ Spice, rubbing the seasoning into the meat 'cuz rubbin' is lovin'. Heat the oil in a heavy frying pan over medium-high heat and sear the chops for about 2 minutes on each side. Remove the chops and set aside.

2. Reduce the heat to medium and add the mushrooms and onion. Sauté for about 10 minutes until tender. Add the garlic; cook, stirring, for 1 minute. Season to taste with salt and pepper. Set aside.

3. Preheat oven to 350°F.

4. In a large greased casserole dish or roasting pan, make an even layer of half of the sliced potatoes. Sprinkle with 1/2 cup of the Parmesan cheese. Spread half of the mushroom mixture evenly over the potatoes. Arrange the pork chops in an even layer over the mushroom mixture. Sprinkle with the herbs. Top with remaining mushroom mixture. Fan the remaining potatoes in a double layer over the top.

5. In a bowl, combine the cream, stock and salt and pepper to taste. Pour over pork the chops. The liquid should come to the top layer of potatoes; if not, add a little more stock and cream. Bake, covered, for 1 hour.

6. Uncover and bake for another 30 to 45 minutes, until the pork chops and potatoes are tender. Sprinkle with the remaining 1/2 cup of Parmesan cheese and brown lightly under the broiler. Let stand for 10 minutes.

7. Serve with steamed fresh peas or green beans.

Serves 8

Bourbon-Braised Lamb Shanks with Mushrooms, Onions and Bacon

My favourite comfort food is lamb shanks. I prefer lamb hind shanks over fore shanks because they are larger and meatier (but they are harder to get).

8 slices bacon	2 cups Really Good Beef Stock (see page 70)
6 large lamb hind shanks	1 cup bourbon
1/2 cup Bone Dust BBQ Spice (see page 42)	2 tbsp. chopped fresh rosemary
1/2 cup all-purpose flour	1 bay leaf
6 cloves garlic, minced	2 tbsp. butter, cut in pieces
6 large shallots, quartered lengthwise	1 tbsp. chopped fresh parsley
6 plum tomatoes, quartered lengthwise	1 tsp. chopped fresh thyme
2 large onions, cut into 1-inch pieces	1 tbsp. balsamic vinegar
3 cups sliced mushrooms	Salt and pepper

1. Preheat oven to 325°F.
2. In a large frying pan over medium heat, fry the bacon until crisp. Remove bacon and set aside. Increase heat to medium-high.
3. Rub the shanks with the Bone Dust BBQ Spice; dredge in the flour. Sear the shanks on all sides in the bacon fat. Transfer shanks to a large roasting pan. Add the bacon, garlic, shallots, tomatoes, onions, mushrooms, stock, bourbon, rosemary and bay leaf. Braise, covered, until tender, 2 1/2 to 3 hours.
4. Transfer shanks to a serving platter. Skim excess fat from pan. In the roasting pan, bring the sauce to a boil. Reduce heat and stir in butter until melted. Stir in parsley, thyme and vinegar. Season to taste with salt and pepper. Discard the bay leaf.
5. Serve shanks with Planked Polenta (see page 126) and drizzle with the sauce.

Serves 6

Oven-Roasted Rack of Lamb Crusted with Dijon, Goat Cheese and Macadamia Nuts

I like to pair my lamb with rich and creamy goat cheese and those most expensive macadamia nuts. This is a special-occasion recipe for that anniversary, birthday or "wanna get some" dinner party.

6 oz. goat cheese

1/2 cup chopped macadamia nuts

1/4 cup dry bread crumbs

2 tbsp. Dijon mustard

1 tbsp. chopped fresh rosemary

Salt and pepper to taste

1 rack of lamb (with 8 bones)

2 tbsp. Bone Dust BBQ Spice (see page 42)

2 tbsp. vegetable oil

1. In a bowl, blend together the goat cheese, nuts, bread crumbs, mustard, rosemary, salt and pepper. Refrigerate until needed.
2. Preheat oven to 425°F.
3. Rub the lamb with the Bone Dust BBQ Spice. In a heavy oven-proof frying pan (I like cast-iron), heat the oil over medium-high heat. Add the lamb, meat side down, and cook for 3 minutes or until nicely golden brown. Turn the rack over and transfer the pan to the oven. Roast for 12 to 15 minutes for medium-rare.
4. Smear the meat side with the cheese mixture. Return to the oven for 2 minutes or until the cheese is soft and the nuts are toasted and brown. Let rest for 5 minutes. Slice the rack into double-boned chops and serve immediately.

Serves 4

Roast Leg of Lamb with Minted Mango Sauce

This minted mango sauce beats mint jelly any day of the week. The aroma through your home from a leg of lamb is truly heavenly.

4 cloves garlic, minced	1 medium shallot, diced
3 tbsp. olive oil	1 large ripe mango, peeled and diced
1 tbsp. minced fresh ginger	1/4 cup dry sherry
1 tbsp. kosher salt	1/4 cup water
1 tbsp. freshly ground black pepper	2 tbsp. sugar
1 bone-in leg of lamb (5 to 6 lb.)	1 tbsp. sherry vinegar
12 mini red potatoes, halved	1 tbsp. chopped fresh mint
2 large carrots, cut into 2-inch-long sticks	Pinch curry powder
1 cup peeled pearl onions	Salt and pepper
6 sprigs fresh mint	

1. Preheat oven to 425°F.
2. In a bowl, combine the garlic, 2 tbsp. of the oil, the ginger, salt and pepper. Mix to form a paste. Make a few shallow slashes in the lamb and rub the lamb all over with the paste, pressing it into the meat. Place lamb on a rack in a roasting pan. Roast for 30 minutes.
3. Arrange the potatoes, carrots and pearl onions around the leg of lamb. Cover the lamb with mint sprigs. Reduce heat to 325°F and roast lamb for 20 minutes per pound (1 1/2 to 2 hours) or until desired doneness. (A meat thermometer will read 150 to 160°F for medium.) Let rest for 10 minutes.
4. While the lamb roasts, prepare the sauce. In a medium saucepan, heat the remaining 1 tbsp. of oil over medium-high heat. Add the shallots; sauté until tender, about 1 minute. Stir in the mango, sherry, water, sugar and sherry vinegar. Bring to a boil, stirring occasionally, for 10 minutes, until thick. Remove from heat and stir in mint, curry powder, and salt and pepper to taste.
5. Carve lamb and serve with the Minted Mango Sauce.

Serves 6 to 8

Mile-High Shepherd's Pie

Layer upon layer of meaty goodness. Use a deep casserole dish to make this dish a mile-high winner.

3 lb. ground lamb

2 tbsp. Bone Dust BBQ Spice (see page 42)

1 tbsp. + 2 tsp. salt

1 tbsp. hot dry mustard

2 tsp. ground cumin

1/2 tsp. ground cinnamon

12 cloves garlic, minced

1/4 cup vegetable oil

1 medium onion, diced

1 small leek, diced

2 medium carrots, diced

3/4 cup fresh or thawed frozen corn kernels

3/4 cup fresh or thawed frozen sweet peas

1/4 cup + 1 tbsp. chopped fresh herbs (such as parsley, rosemary, thyme)

Salt and pepper to taste

1 cup crumbled goat cheese

1 1/2 lb. mini red potatoes

1/2 cup sour cream

1/4 cup grated Parmesan cheese

3 tbsp. butter

1/2 cup reduced Really Good Beef Stock (see page 70) or lamb demi-glace

6 slices challah, cut into 1/2-inch cubes

1. In a large bowl, mix together the lamb, Bone Dust BBQ Spice, 1 tbsp. of the salt, the mustard, cumin, cinnamon and garlic.

2. Heat 2 tbsp. of the oil in a large, heavy frying pan over medium-high heat. Sauté the lamb, in small batches, until fully cooked, adding more oil as necessary. Drain and set aside.

3. In the same pan, cook the onions, stirring, for 5 to 8 minutes, until browned and tender. Add the leek and carrots; sauté for 5 minutes more. Remove from heat. Stir in the corn, peas, 1 tbsp. of the herbs, and salt and pepper. Gently fold in 1/2 cup of the goat cheese. Set aside.

4. Preheat oven to 400°F.

5. In a large saucepan, cover the potatoes with cold water. Bring to a rolling boil. Add salt, reduce heat and simmer for 10 to 15 minutes, until tender. Drain potatoes and return to pot over high heat, shaking the pan until potatoes are dry. Mash the potatoes. Add sour cream, Parmesan cheese, butter and salt and pepper to taste. Mix well. Set aside.

6. Spoon the lamb into a 4-inch-deep casserole dish. Pour the reduced stock over the meat. Spread the vegetable mixture over the meat. Top with the mashed potatoes, spreading evenly.

7. In a bowl, combine challah, remaining 1/2 cup of goat cheese, remaining 1/4 cup of herbs, and salt and pepper to taste. Spread over the mashed potatoes. Cover loosely with foil. Bake until hot, 30 to 40 minutes.

8. Remove foil. Return to oven to brown, about 5 minutes. Let rest 10 minutes before serving.

Serves 6 to 8

Veal Chops with Capers and Balsamic Vinegar

I like to purchase Provimi white veal chops instead of red veal. White veal is milk fed, so the flavour is sweet and the meat tender. No marinating to tenderize is required for white veal.

4 veal rib chops (each 1 lb. and about 1 1/2 inches thick)

2 tbsp. Amazing Steak Spice (see page 43)

2 tbsp. olive oil

2 cloves garlic, minced

3 medium shallots, sliced

2 tbsp. rinsed and drained large capers, chopped

1/4 cup aged balsamic vinegar

2 tbsp. cold butter

2 tbsp. chopped fresh basil

Salt and pepper

8 oz. double- or triple-crème Brie cheese

1. Preheat broiler.
2. Season the chops with the Amazing Steak Spice, pressing the spices into the meat. Place chops on a broiler pan. Broil the chops, with the oven door slightly open, 2 to 3 inches below the heat, until lightly browned, 3 to 5 minutes. Turn chops over and broil for 3 to 5 minutes more for medium-rare (a meat thermometer should read 150°F).
3. While the chops are broiling, prepare the sauce. In a medium saucepan, heat the oil over high heat. Sauté the garlic and shallots until tender, about 1 minute. Stir in the capers. Remove from heat and add balsamic vinegar and butter. Stir until the butter is incorporated. Stir in the basil and salt and pepper to taste.
4. Spoon a few tablespoons of the sauce over each chop and top with a slice or two of Brie. Serve with couscous and kohlrabi.

Serves 4

Veal Osso Buco with Lots of Stuff

When I make osso buco, I love to cook it low and slow for hours. I love braised slow-cooked food, especially on Sundays, when I can watch the latest race and have a few pints. And don't forget to eat the marrow from the centre of the bones. Spread it on toast!

1/4 cup all-purpose flour	3 tbsp. Dijon mustard
1 tbsp. Bone Dust BBQ Spice (see page 42)	2 tbsp. chopped fresh herbs (such as thyme, oregano,
6 veal shanks (each 12 to 16 oz. and 2 inches thick)	basil, flat-leaf parsley)
1/4 cup olive oil	2 tbsp. hot prepared horseradish
8 cloves garlic, minced	Salt and pepper
1 large onion, finely diced	1/4 cup cognac
2 stalks celery, finely diced	3 cups Really Good Beef Stock (see page 70) or veal stock
3 large carrots, finely diced	6 cups mashed potatoes
3 cups torn oyster mushrooms	1/2 cup sour cream
2 cups diced butternut squash	2 tbsp. chopped fresh chives

1. Preheat oven to 250°F.
2. In a large plastic bag, combine the flour and Bone Dust BBQ Spice. Shake to mix. Add veal shanks and shake to evenly coat the meat.
3. Heat the oil in a large, heavy frying pan over medium-high heat. Brown the veal on both sides. Remove from pan and set aside.
4. Add a little more oil to the pan if necessary. Add the garlic and onions; sauté for 2 to 3 minutes, until tender. Add the celery, carrots, mushrooms and squash; sauté for 3 to 5 minutes, until lightly browned. Remove from heat and stir in the mustard, herbs, horseradish, and salt and pepper to taste. Spread the vegetable mixture evenly in a roasting pan. Stir in the cognac and beef stock. The mixture should be a little soupy and not too thick; add a little extra stock if necessary.
5. Press the veal shanks into the vegetable mixture so that the meat and vegetables are the same level. Cover. Braise, stirring occasionally, for 4 to 5 hours, until the meat easily falls from the bones. Add more liquid if too much has evaporated.
6. Place a scoop of the mashed potatoes on each plate and top with osso buco. Top with braised vegetable mixture and sauce. Garnish with sour cream and fresh chives.

Serves 6

Pan-Fried Veal Liver Nuggets
with Double-Smoked Bacon, Pears and Pearl Onions

When I was a kid, I hated liver. My mom used to make it taste like my shoe. Veal liver is delicate and tender, and no liver should be overcooked. Ask your butcher to cut you a piece of veal liver between 1 and 1 1/2 inches thick and weighing about 1 pound. The thicker liver isn't as easy to overcook.

8 slices thick-cut bacon, cut into 1/2-inch pieces
1 cup peeled and halved pearl onions
1 lb. veal liver, trimmed of outer membrane and veins
1/4 cup all-purpose flour
1 tbsp. Bone Dust BBQ Spice (see page 42)
2 tbsp. butter
1 Bosc pear, peeled and diced
2 tbsp. chopped fresh chives
Squeeze lemon juice
Salt and pepper

1. In a large, heavy frying pan over medium-high heat, sauté the bacon until lightly browned and crisp. Transfer bacon to a bowl and set aside.
2. In the bacon fat, fry the pearl onions for 4 to 6 minutes, until browned and tender. Add to bacon.
3. Cut the liver into 2-inch chunks. Place the liver nuggets in a bowl and add the flour and Bone Dust BBQ Spice. Toss to evenly coat.
4. In the same pan, melt the butter over high heat. Add the liver, a few pieces at a time, and fry, turning, until brown on all sides. Add the bacon, onions and pears; gently stir until heated. Stir in chives, lemon juice, and salt and pepper to taste.
5. Serve immediately with rice or boiled potatoes.

Serves 4 to 6

Double-Boned Venison Chops with Indian Spices and Fuzzy Peach Cilantro Sauce

Venison is a very lean meat: be careful not to overcook it! Venison chops are best eaten rare to medium.

6 double-boned venison chops (each 8 to 10 oz.)

3 tbsp. Cochin Curry Masala Seasoning (see page 46)

2 tbsp. vegetable oil

2 tbsp. butter

1/2 cup golden raisins, soaked in warm water for 20 minutes and drained

1/2 cup shaved fresh coconut

Fuzzy Peach Cilantro Sauce

2 ripe peaches

1 medium shallot, chopped

1 small hot green chili

Juice of 1 lime

3 cups fresh cilantro leaves

2 tbsp. peach schnapps

2 tbsp. olive oil

1 tbsp. minced fresh ginger

1 tsp. Cochin Curry Masala Seasoning (see page 46)

1 tsp. sugar

1. Preheat oven to 350°F.
2. Season the chops with the Cochin Curry Masala Seasoning, pressing the spices into the meat. Set aside.
3. To make the Fuzzy Peach Cilantro Sauce, blanch the peaches in a pot of boiling water for 2 to 3 minutes. Cool under cold running water, then peel. Cut the peaches into large wedges. In a food processor, combine the peaches, shallot, chili, lime juice, cilantro, peach schnapps, olive oil, ginger, Cochin Curry Masala Seasoning and sugar. Process until smooth. Transfer to a bowl and chill.
4. Heat the vegetable oil in a large frying pan over high heat. Sear the venison chops for 1 to 2 minutes, turning to brown on both sides. Transfer to a baking sheet and roast for 8 to 10 minutes for rare to medium-rare. Remove from oven and let rest, covered loosely with foil.
5. In the same pan that you seared the venison in, melt the butter over high heat. Add the raisins and coconut. Stir until heated through. Remove from heat and stir into the Fuzzy Peach Cilantro Sauce. Slice each venison chop in half and serve with the sauce.

Serves 6

Note: To prepare the coconut, skewer one of the three eyes in the end and drain the liquid. Heat the coconut in a 400°F oven for 15 minutes. Hit it with a hammer or mallet to break the shell. With a dull knife, separate the white meat from the shell. Use a grater or food processor to shave the coconut.

Smokin' Buffalo Ribs

While in Richmond, British Columbia, I met a couple of guys who own the restaurant Dem Bones. I had the treat of eating their awesome buffalo ribs. Here's my version.

1 tbsp. Bayou Bite Cajun Rub (see page 44)

2 tbsp. kosher salt

2 meaty buffalo ribs (each 2 to 3 lb.)

1 large onion, sliced

1 1/2 bottles dark ale

1/4 cup butter, melted

1/4 cup honey

1/4 cup Louisiana-style hot sauce (such as Durkee's Red Hot)

2 tbsp. chipotle Tabasco sauce

2 tbsp. ketchup

1. Preheat oven to 325°F.
2. In a medium bowl, combine the salt and Bayou Bite Cajun Rub. Rub the buffalo ribs with the spice mixture, pressing the spices into the meat so they adhere. Spread the onion slices in a roasting pan. Top with the ribs. Add the beer. Cover and roast until the meat is tender and the bones can be easily pulled from the meat, 2 1/2 to 3 hours.
3. Drain beer and fat from the onions and transfer the onions to a large bowl. Slice ribs between every bone and add to the onions. Add the butter, honey, Louisiana hot sauce, Tabasco and ketchup. Toss to coat.
4. Return ribs and onions to the roasting pan, spreading evenly. Roast, uncovered, until hot, sticky and crispy, about 15 minutes. Serve with loads of napkins.

Serves 4 to 8

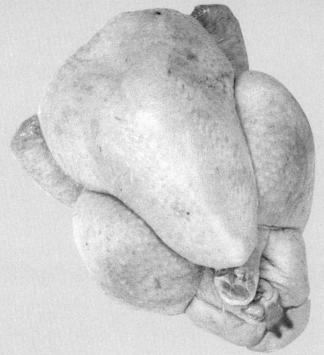
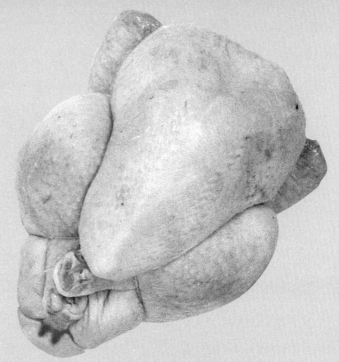

Recipes for birds

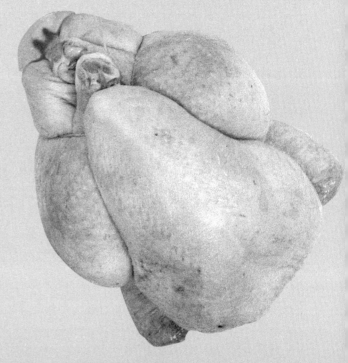

His Oven-Roasted Drunken Beer Can Chicken

Beer Can Chicken, Drunken Chicken, Beer Butt Chicken or whatever you want to call it, this is the best bird on the grill. But it rocks in the oven too. Men and beer. Need I say more?

1/4 cup butter
1/2 cup BBQ sauce
1/4 cup maple syrup
1 tbsp. chipotle chili in adobo sauce, puréed
1/4 cup beer
1 chicken (3 to 4 lb.)
1/4 cup Bone Dust BBQ Spice (see page 42)
1 tall boy (16 oz./455 mL) beer

1. Preheat oven to 375°F. Set an oven rack on the lowest level.
2. In a small saucepan over medium heat, melt the butter. Add the BBQ sauce, maple syrup, chili and 1/4 cup of beer. Stir until heated. Remove from heat and set aside.
3. Wash the chicken inside and out with cold water and pat dry with paper towels. Rub chicken inside and out with the Bone Dust BBQ Spice, pressing the seasoning into the meat so it adheres. Open the beer can. Take a big sip out of the beer because you want to. Go on, take another. Oh hell, drink the damn beer and open another. Now you still have to take a sip from the second can. Put the can upright in a roasting pan and stand the chicken on it. Yeah, that's right, the can goes up inside.
4. Roast the chicken, basting liberally with the maple BBQ sauce, for 20 minutes per pound (1 to 1 1/4 hours), or until the chicken is fully cooked (a meat thermometer inserted in the thigh will read 160°F).
5. Hold the chicken firmly with a pair of tongs, and with your free hand, use a carving fork to skewer the chicken in the breast, then carefully pull it up off the can. Carve chicken and serve with extra maple chipotle BBQ sauce.

Serves 4 to 6

Her Oven-Roasted Garlic Herb Wine Chicken on a Can

For all the wonderful women out there, here's something a little more refined than the usual Beer Butt Chicken. Enjoy!

1 can (16 oz./455 mL) beer

2 cups dry white wine

1 chicken (3 to 4 lb.)

4 tbsp. Garlic Herb Steak Paste (see page 47)

4 sprigs mixed fresh herbs (parsley, sage, rosemary, thyme, tarragon, oregano)

2 cloves garlic, minced

1/4 cup butter

1/2 cup honey

1. Preheat oven to 375°F. Set an oven rack on the lowest level. Pour out a glass of beer for yourself and your mate, then rinse the empty can. Pour 1 1/2 cups of the wine into the can.
2. Wash the chicken inside and out with cold water and pat dry with paper towels. Rub chicken inside and out with 3 tbsp. of the Garlic Herb Steak Paste, pressing the seasoning into the meat so it adheres. Stuff the beer can with the herb sprigs and garlic and put the can in a roasting pan. Place the chicken over the beer can so that the can is in the cavity and the bird is standing upright. Press firmly to set well. Arrange the chicken legs so they cross in front of the can.
3. In a small saucepan over medium heat, melt the butter. Stir in the remaining 1/2 cup of wine, the honey and remaining 1 tbsp. of steak paste. Stir until mixed and heated through. Remove from heat and set aside.
4. Roast the chicken, basting liberally with the honey sauce, for 20 minutes per pound (1 to 1 1/4 hours), or until the chicken is fully cooked (a meat thermometer inserted in the thigh will read 160°F).
5. Hold the chicken firmly with a pair of tongs, and with your free hand, use a carving fork to skewer the chicken in the breast, then carefully pull it up off the can. Carve chicken and serve drizzled with extra honey sauce.

Serves 4 to 6

Cedar-Planked Honeycomb Chicken Breasts

The combination of the plank and the honeycomb makes this stuffed chicken delicate and delicious, perfect for parties, quiet family dinners or one of those meals to help you get some good lovin'.

2 green onions, roughly chopped

1/2 cup 1/2-inch pieces of honeycomb

1/2 cup grated Romano cheese

1/4 cup butter, softened

2 tbsp. chopped fresh thyme

4 boneless skinless chicken breasts (each 6 to 8 oz.)

2 to 3 cups dry white wine

1/2 cup peanuts, crushed

2 tsp. Bone Dust BBQ Spice (see page 42)

Special equipment: 1 untreated cedar plank (at least 8 × 12 inches and 1 inch thick), soaked in cold water for at least 1 hour

1. In a bowl, using a fork, mash the green onions, honeycomb, Romano cheese, butter and thyme into a coarse mixture. Working with 2 tbsp. of the honeycomb butter at a time, shape four balls; press to flatten. Freeze patties on a plate for 1 hour. Set aside remaining honeycomb butter at room temperature.

2. Preheat oven to 450°F.

3. Cut away the chicken tenderloins and cut out the tough tendon. Lay the tenderloins between two sheets of plastic wrap and gently pound until 1/4 inch thick; set aside. Using a sharp knife, cut a pocket about 1 inch deep from the top to the bottom of each breast. Using your fingers, carefully push the meat apart to make a large pocket.

4. Place a frozen patty in each chicken cavity. Place a flattened tenderloin over the cavity and tuck the tenderloin into the opening, firmly pressing the edges to make a tight seal.

5. Place the plank in a deep baking dish large enough to hold it. Pour the wine around the plank until it floats. Heat plank in oven for 10 minutes or until you can smell the cedar.

6. In a small bowl, combine the peanuts and Bone Dust BBQ Spice. Rub the top of each chicken breast with 1 tsp. of the reserved honeycomb butter and coat with the peanut mixture, carefully pressing the nuts so they adhere. Carefully place chicken on the plank. Bake for 30 minutes or until the chicken is cooked through, checking the liquid level every 10 minutes and adding more wine or water if the pan looks dry.

7. Top each serving of chicken with a dollop of reserved honeycomb butter. Cut into the centre of the chicken breast and watch the honeycomb butter ooze sweet goodness. Marvellous!

Serves 4

Suicide Chicken Wings

I like many things in life to be spicy. My meats, my condiments, my women and my buffalo-style chicken wings. If you have sinus congestion or a masochistic need to burn your face off, then this is the dish for you. Have lots of tissues, napkins and antacids on hand. Fabulous!

4 lb. chicken wings, halved at joint

1/4 cup Bayou Bite Cajun Rub (see page 44)

1 tbsp. vegetable oil

1 small onion, finely chopped

2 to 3 Scotch bonnet peppers, seeded and minced

2 green onions, thinly sliced

1 cup hot and spicy BBQ sauce

1/2 cup honey

1 tbsp. Worcestershire sauce

1 tbsp. chopped fresh cilantro

Salt and pepper

1. Rinse the chicken wings under cold running water and pat dry with paper towels. Put the wings in a large bowl and add the Cajun Rub. With your hands, toss the wings in the spice to evenly coat, pressing the spices into the meat. Cover and refrigerate for 2 hours.

2. Preheat oven to 425°F. Line a baking sheet with foil. Arrange the wings on the baking sheet and bake in the upper third of the oven for 30 to 40 minutes, turning once, until crispy, golden brown and fully cooked.

3. Meanwhile, make the Suicide Sauce. Heat the oil in a medium saucepan over medium heat. Fry the onion, peppers and green onions for 3 to 5 minutes, stirring. Stir in the BBQ sauce, honey and Worcestershire sauce; bring to a boil. Reduce heat and simmer, stirring occasionally, for 5 minutes. Remove from heat. Stir in the cilantro and season with salt and pepper to taste.

4. Transfer wings to a large bowl and toss with Suicide Sauce. Return to baking sheet and cook for 10 to 15 minutes more, until chicken is fully cooked and sticky. Serve with Smoky Bacon Blue Cheese Dip (see page 53).

Serves 4

Gospel Southern Skillet-Fried Sour Cream Chicken

Bless this chicken: it's divine, delicious and heavenly. The sour cream helps to tenderize the chicken and allows the flour to adhere, making a crispy golden crust.

2 cups sour cream

1 tbsp. chopped fresh sage

1 tbsp. + 2 tsp. Bone Dust BBQ Spice (see page 42)

1 tbsp. lemon juice

1 chicken (3 to 4 lb.)

2 cups all-purpose flour

1/2 lb. shortening

1. In a large bowl, whisk together the sour cream, sage, 1 tbsp. of the Bone Dust BBQ Spice and the lemon juice.
2. Rinse the chicken under cold running water and pat dry with paper towels. Using a sharp knife, cut chicken into 10 parts: two wings, two thighs, two drumsticks and two breasts, then cut each breast in half. Add chicken parts to sour cream mixture and stir to coat completely. Marinate, covered and refrigerated, for 4 to 6 hours or overnight.
3. In a large bowl, stir together the flour and remaining 2 tsp. Bone Dust BBQ Spice.
4. In a large 3-inch-deep cast-iron pan, melt the shortening over medium heat. (When melted the shortening should be 1/2 to 3/4 inch deep.) Heat the shortening to 350°F.
5. Starting with the largest pieces of chicken, and working with one piece at a time, remove chicken from marinade and roll in seasoned flour to coat well. Slowly add the chicken to the shortening. Repeat with remaining chicken, working in batches if necessary so you don't crowd the pan. Fry the chicken for 8 to 10 minutes on one side, or until golden brown and crisp. Turn over and continue to cook until fully cooked, golden brown and crisp, 15 to 20 minutes, depending on the size of the chicken. Drain on paper towels.
6. Serve immediately with fried green tomatoes, Colonel Mustard's Slaw (see page 109) and Banditos Baked Beans (see page 223).

Serves 3 to 4

Wine Country Chicken Steam à Sauté with Grapes, Gruyère and Cream

A steam à sauté makes everything tender and yummy. It's so comforting to cook in one pan. Be sure to have some bread on hand for sopping up the sauce.

4 boneless skin-on chicken breasts (each 5 to 8 oz.)

2 tbsp. Garlic Herb Steak Paste (see page 47)

2 tbsp. olive oil

1 tbsp. butter

1/4 cup finely chopped shallots

1/2 cup Riesling

1/2 cup heavy cream

1 cup halved seedless green grapes

1/2 cup cubed Gruyère cheese

Salt and pepper

1. Rub the chicken with the steak paste. Marinate, covered and refrigerated, for 1 hour.
2. In a 2-inch-deep sauté pan, heat the oil over medium-high heat. Fry the chicken, skin side down, for 1 to 2 minutes, or until seared. Turn and sear the other side. Remove the chicken from the pan.
3. Melt the butter in the pan. Sauté the shallots for 1 to 2 minutes, until tender. Return chicken to the pan. Add the Riesling and bring to a boil, stirring up the crispy bits from the bottom of the pan. Add the cream. Bring to a boil, reduce heat to medium and cover. Steam-sauté for 8 to 10 minutes, until chicken is fully cooked and the sauce is thick.
4. Add the grapes and cheese; gently stir until the sauce is thick and the cheese is gooey. Season to taste with salt and pepper. Serve the chicken with lots of sauce.

Serves 4

Cajun Blackened BBQ Skillet Chicken with Crawfish Butter

I had a dish similar to this while I was partying one night in a tiny place off Bourbon Street, in New Orleans. For the life of me I can't remember the name of the place. Must have been the bourbon. But I do remember the chicken—tender and spicy and topped with lots of crawfish meat in a buttery sauce. You can find frozen crawfish tail meat in specialty seafood stores, usually in 1-lb. blocks.

4 large chicken legs

1/2 cup + 2 tbsp. butter, softened

3 tbsp. Bayou Bite Cajun Rub (see page 44)

1 cup crawfish tail meat, thawed and drained

1/4 cup chopped fresh chives

1 tbsp. lemon juice

Dash hot sauce

Salt and pepper

1. With a sharp knife, cut a ring 1 1/2 inches down from the top of each drumstick to release the skin from the bone. Lay the leg skin side down, and make a deep incision along the length of, and down to, the bone. Cut around the bone and joint, carefully separating the meat from the bone but keeping the meat in one piece. (Freeze the bones for making stock.)

2. Place a boneless leg between two sheets of plastic wrap. Using the flat side of a meat mallet or a rolling pin, pound the meat to a thickness of 3/4 to 1 inch. Repeat with remaining legs.

3. Melt 2 tbsp. of the butter. Brush both sides of the chicken legs with the butter. Rub the chicken liberally with the Bayou Bite Cajun Rub. Chill, covered, while you prepare the crawfish butter.

4. In a large bowl, combine the remaining 1/2 cup of butter, the crawfish meat, chives and lemon juice. Season with a dash of hot sauce and salt and pepper to taste. Mix well. Set aside.

5. In a well-ventilated kitchen, heat a large dry frying pan over medium-high heat until it begins to smoke. Working in batches if necessary, cook the legs, skin side down, for 3 to 5 minutes, until golden brown. Turn and cook for another 3 to 5 minutes or until cooked through.

6. Serve topped with a dollop or two of crawfish butter.

Serves 4

White Trash Chicken à la King of the Q

This trailer-trash fare—one of my favourites—requires that the chicken breasts marinate for 24 hours. In beer. That's why it's one of my favourites.

6 boneless skinless chicken breasts (each 6 to 8 oz.)

1 bottle + 1/2 cup dark beer

1 1/2 cups Really Good Béchamel Sauce (see page 74)

1/2 cup ranch dressing

1/2 cup heavy cream

2 tbsp. Bone Dust BBQ Spice (see page 42)

1 tbsp. vegetable oil

6 slices bacon, diced

1 large sweet onion, diced

3 cloves garlic, minced

1 jalapeño pepper, seeded and chopped

2 cups quartered button mushrooms

2 cups frozen mixed peas, corn and carrots

1 can (14 oz./398 mL) lima beans, rinsed and drained

1/2 cup shredded Monterey Jack cheese

1/2 cup crushed tortilla chips

1. Marinate chicken in 1 bottle of the beer, covered and refrigerated, for 24 hours.

2. Preheat grill to medium-high. Stir together the béchamel, ranch dressing and cream. Set aside.

3. Remove chicken from marinade, discarding the marinade. Rub chicken with Bone Dust BBQ Spice. Brush chicken lightly with the oil. Grill for 6 to 8 minutes per side or until fully cooked. Let cool. Cut chicken into 1-inch chunks; set aside.

4. Preheat oven to 350°F.

5. In a large frying pan over medium-high heat, fry the bacon until just crisp. Remove with a slotted spoon and drain on paper towels.

6. In the same pan, sauté the onion in the bacon fat for 3 to 5 minutes, until tender. Add the garlic, jalapeño pepper and mushrooms; sauté for about 8 minutes, until tender. Stir in frozen vegetables, lima beans, the remaining 1/2 cup beer, and the béchamel mixture. Bring to a low boil. Stir in the chicken and bacon.

7. Transfer to a 9-inch-square casserole dish. Bake, uncovered, for 20 to 30 minutes, until browned, heated through and bubbling. Stir together the Monterey Jack and tortilla chips; sprinkle over casserole. Bake for 5 minutes more or until cheese is melted. Let sit for 5 minutes before serving.

Serves 6

Jiffy Peanut BBQ Chicken

Ahh, peanut butter … another one of my favourite things. I eat it on bread, buns, bananas, almost anything—and especially on chicken. Delicious!

2 tbsp. Bone Dust BBQ Spice (see page 42)

4 chicken thighs, trimmed of excess fat

4 chicken drumsticks, trimmed of excess fat

2 tbsp. oil

1/4 cup lager

1 cup BBQ sauce

2 tbsp. Bayou Bite Cajun Rub (see page 44)

2 tbsp. malt vinegar

2 tbsp. crunchy peanut butter

1 tsp. sugar

1 tsp. Worcestershire sauce

3 tbsp. butter

1/4 cup peanuts, crushed

1. Preheat oven to 425°F.
2. Rub the Bone Dust BBQ Spice into the chicken pieces, pressing the spices gently into the meat. In a large frying pan over medium heat, heat the oil. Fry the chicken for 4 minutes per side or until golden brown. Transfer to an 11 × 7-inch baking dish.
3. Drain the fat from the pan and return pan to medium heat. Add the beer, stirring to scrape up any browned bits from the bottom of the pan. Add the BBQ sauce, Cajun Rub, vinegar, peanut butter, sugar and Worcestershire sauce. Bring to a boil, stirring. Pour over chicken. Roast, uncovered, for 25 to 30 minutes or until chicken is fully cooked.
4. Transfer the chicken to serving plates. Stir the butter into the sauce until it is melted. Spoon the sauce over the chicken and sprinkle with crushed peanuts.

Serves 4 to 6

Chicken in a Bag

This dish is simple to prepare but tastes like you spent a whole day slaving away in the kitchen. Your chicken will be juicy, succulent and cooked to perfection. When the accolades come in and people offer you clean-up help, money, etc., I promise I won't tell if you won't.

4 boneless skin-on chicken breasts (each 6 to 8 oz.)
8 tsp. Bayou Bite Cajun Rub (see page 44) or Bone Dust BBQ Spice (see page 42)

1. Preheat oven to 425°F. Heat a pizza stone on the middle rack of the oven, if desired.
2. Place a chicken breast in each of four brown paper "food grade" lunch bags. Add 2 tsp. of the Cajun Rub to each bag and shake to evenly coat chicken. Turn chicken breasts so that they are skin side down in the bottom of each bag. Tightly fold down the top of each bag three or four times to seal it. Don't crush or roll the bags; leave some air inside.
3. Place bags on a cookie sheet or a pizza stone and bake in the middle of the oven for 16 to 20 minutes, until the chicken is fully cooked, tender and moist. Carefully unroll bags to allow the steam to escape.
4. Slice the chicken and serve immediately.

Serves 4

Chicken Chop Chop Suey

More "real Canadian" Chinese food! I like to prepare this dish twice, 'cause you know that an hour after eating it you're going to be hungry for a second round.

2 boneless skinless chicken breasts (each 4 to 6 oz.)

4 1/4 cups Really Good Roasted Chicken Stock (see page 71)

3 tbsp. rice vinegar

1 tsp. salt

3 tbsp. peanut oil or vegetable oil

1 cup thinly sliced shiitake mushrooms

1 small onion, sliced

1 clove garlic, minced

1 tsp. minced fresh ginger

1 stalk celery, thinly sliced diagonally

1 1/2 cups sugar snap peas

1/4 cup pineapple juice

1 tbsp. soy sauce

1 tsp. sambal oelek

2 tsp. tapioca starch

3 cups bean sprouts

Salt and pepper

1. Using a sharp knife, cut the chicken breasts crosswise on a slight angle into 1/2-inch-thick slices. Lightly flatten each slice with your fingers. Set aside.

2. In a large saucepan, bring 4 cups of the stock to a boil. Add 1 tbsp. of the vinegar and the salt. Reduce heat to a low boil. Drop chicken pieces into stock, one at a time. Return to the boil and boil for 1 minute. Drain chicken. Set aside, keeping warm.

3. Heat a wok or large frying pan over high heat until the pan is smoking. Add the oil.

4. Stir-fry the mushrooms for 30 seconds to 1 minute or until tender. Move mushrooms out to the sides of the pan, leaving a well in the middle. Add the onion, garlic and ginger. Stir-fry until tender, about 1 minute. Add the celery, snap peas and the chicken; stir everything together. Add the remaining 1/4 cup of stock, remaining 2 tbsp. of rice vinegar, the pineapple juice, soy sauce and sambal oelek. Bring to a boil, cover and simmer for 1 minute.

5. Dissolve the tapioca starch in a splash of water. Add to the wok and stir until thick. Reduce heat to very low. Stir in bean sprouts, season to taste with salt and pepper, and serve immediately.

Serves 6

Hot-Crossed Stuffed Chick'n Bomb

It's "da bomb, baby"! Particularly good for when you're in the dog house or just feel like getting lucky. Oh, the flavours … the bacon, the chicken, and that bread crumb, arugula and cheese stuffing. Ecstasy!

4 oz. buffalo mozzarella cheese

8 slices thick-cut bacon

2 tbsp. butter

1 small onion, thinly sliced

1 large shallot, minced

2 cloves garlic, minced

1/2 cup thinly sliced roasted red bell pepper

1/4 cup dry white wine

2 cups arugula, washed and drained

1/2 cup grated Parmesan cheese

1/4 cup dry bread crumbs

4 chicken legs

3 tbsp. Bone Dust BBQ Spice (see page 42)

1. Cut the mozzarella into four equal cubes. Freeze for 30 minutes.
2. In a frying pan over medium-high heat, cook the bacon until the fat is rendered but the bacon is still pliable. Drain on paper towels and set aside.
3. Drain the fat from the pan and melt the butter over medium-high heat. Add the onion and cook, stirring, for 3 to 4 minutes or until softened. Add the shallot, garlic and red pepper; cook, stirring, for another minute. Add the wine. Bring to a boil and reduce the liquid by half. Add the arugula, Parmesan cheese and bread crumbs; toss well. Remove from heat, transfer to a bowl and let cool slightly. The mixture should be thick enough that you can form it into a loose ball. If the mixture is too wet, add a little more Parmesan. Divide the mixture in half and set aside.
4. Preheat oven to 400°F. Line a baking sheet with foil.
5. With a sharp knife, cut a ring 1 1/2 inches down from the top of each drumstick to release the skin from the bone. Lay the leg skin side down, and make a deep incision along the length of, and down to, the bone. Cut around the bone and joint, carefully separating the meat from the bone but keeping the meat in one piece. (Freeze the bones for making stock.)

6. On a cutting board, crisscross bacon to make four X shapes. Rub the chicken on all sides with the Bone Dust BBQ Spice. Using half of the arugula stuffing, place an equal amount in the centre of each leg. Place a frozen cheese cube on the stuffing and cover evenly with the other half of the arugula stuffing. Working with one leg at a time, bring the corners up to the centre, creating a ball. Overlap the edges and pull the skin tight to create a seal. Place the stuffed breast, skin side down, on one of the bacon crosses. Stretch the ends of the bacon over the chicken ball. Keeping the ball tight, flip it back over to reveal the cross. Transfer chicken to the baking sheet. Repeat with remaining chicken balls.

7. Roast for 25 to 30 minutes or until you see the cheese melting outwards. Let rest for 2 minutes before serving.

Serves 4

Dad's Turkey with Savory Stuffing, Screech Partridgeberry Relish and Pan Gravy

My dad makes a delicious holiday turkey. He doesn't cook a lot, but this turkey rocks. We have it three or four times a year. Brining the turkey tenderizes it and keeps the meat moist. Try apple juice or beer instead of water for added flavour.

The Turkey

1 turkey (15 to 18 lb.), with neck and giblets (heart, liver and gizzard)

4 quarts water

2 cups kosher salt

Special equipment: a large bucket, pot or container that will hold the turkey and fit in the refrigerator

The Stuffing

2 to 3 loaves stale enriched white bread

2 medium onions

2 stalks celery (optional)

3/4 lb. butter, melted

Dried savory (preferably Newfoundland) or dried sage to taste

Salt and pepper to taste

1 green or McIntosh apple

The Gravy

2 cups Really Good Roasted Chicken Stock (see page 71), turkey stock or reserved cooking water from potatoes, cabbage or carrots

1 tbsp. cornstarch

Salt and pepper

Day 1

1. Remove neck and giblets from the turkey; set giblets aside, refrigerated. Rinse turkey under cold running water. Place the neck in the body cavity and place the turkey in the bucket. Combine the water and salt, stirring until salt is dissolved, and pour over the turkey. (Add more water if necessary to completely cover the turkey, adding 1 tbsp. of salt for every additional cup of water.) Brine the turkey, covered and refrigerated (or, as my dad does, put it in the garage in the cold winter months), for 24 hours

2. Prepare the Screech Partridgeberry Relish (recipe follows).

3. To get a head start on the stuffing, cut the crusts from the bread. Cut or tear the bread into 1-inch pieces. Place in a large bowl and allow to dry overnight. Dice the onions and celery (if using); stir together in a bowl, cover and refrigerate. Get a good night's sleep because the next day is the biggie.

Day 2

1. If you're like my dad, you'll be up at about 5 or 6 to get the turkey ready and into the oven. Remove the turkey from the brine, discarding brine, and remove the neck from the turkey; set neck aside. Rinse the turkey under cold water and pat dry with paper towels.

2. Preheat oven to 425°F.

3. Prepare the stuffing. To the onions and celery, add the bread cubes, melted butter, savory, salt and pepper. Stir well to moisten.

4. Stuff the turkey, packing the stuffing firmly but being careful not to overstuff and saving some stuffing for the neck. Place the apple in the opening of the turkey to fill the hole and secure with skewers. Press the drumsticks to the body and tie the legs together with kitchen string. Fill the neck cavity with stuffing. Pull excess skin over the stuffing and secure with skewers.

5. Place the turkey, breast side up, on a rack in a roasting pan. Add neck and giblets to the pan. Cover turkey loosely with foil, shiny side down, and roast for 30 minutes. Reduce temperature to 325°F and roast turkey, covered with foil and basting occasionally with pan juices, for 20 minutes per pound (5 to 6 hours total), until fully cooked. (A meat thermometer inserted in the thickest part of the thigh should read at least 170°F.) Remove foil during the last 30 minutes of cooking time to allow the turkey to brown.

6. Reduce temperature to 200°F. Carefully lift the turkey onto a serving platter. Cover with foil and then with several kitchen towels to keep the turkey warm. Allow the turkey to rest while you make the gravy.

The Gravy

Drain excess fat from the pan juices. Heat the roasting pan over medium, scraping the browned bits from the bottom of the pan. Add the stock. Bring to a boil, stirring. Dissolve the cornstarch in a little water; stir into boiling broth. Cook, stirring, until the gravy begins to thicken. Reduce heat and simmer, stirring frequently, until thickened. Season to taste with salt and pepper. Set aside, keeping warm.

To Carve

1. Spoon all of the stuffing into a bowl and keep warm in the oven. Carve the bird by first cutting off the breasts, then the legs, and lastly munch the wings.

2. Serve turkey, stuffing and gravy with Screech Partridgeberry Relish (see below).
Serves a hearty family with leftovers for great sandwiches the next day

Screech Partridgeberry Relish

2 cups Newfoundland partridgeberries	1/4 cup Screech
3/4 cup sugar	1/4 cup orange juice

In a medium saucepan, stir together berries, sugar, Screech and orange juice. Bring slowly to a rolling boil, stirring occasionally. Reduce heat to low, cover and simmer for 15 minutes, stirring occasionally, until thickened. Skim froth, if necessary, and let cool. Refrigerate until needed.

Oven Q'ed BBQ Turkey Ribs

Turkey ribs? Not really. They're actually thighs, but "ribs" just sound better.

8 turkey thighs (each 8 to 10 oz.)
2 to 3 tbsp. Amazing Steak Spice (see page 43)
4 cloves garlic, crushed
1 medium onion, sliced
1 tart apple (Mutsu or McIntosh), sliced into 1/2-inch wedges
1/4 cup fresh sage leaves, coarsely chopped
2 cups hard apple cider, apple cider or apple juice
1/2 cup BBQ sauce
2 tbsp. apple butter

1. Preheat oven to 325°F.
2. Trim the turkey thighs of excess skin and fat. Rub thighs with the Amazing Steak Spice, pressing the seasonings into the meat.
3. In a baking dish, toss together the garlic, onion, apple and sage. Spread evenly in the dish. Place the turkey thighs on the apple mixture. Pour in 1 1/2 cups of the cider. Cover tightly with foil. Braise thighs for 1 1/2 hours or until tender and fully cooked.
4. Transfer thighs to a foil-lined baking sheet. Increase oven temperature to 425°F.
5. Strain the apple mixture, reserving pan juices. In a blender, combine the apple mixture, the remaining 1/2 cup of cider, the BBQ sauce and apple butter; purée until smooth. If the mixture is too thick, add a little of the pan juices. Transfer sauce to a small saucepan and warm over medium-low heat, stirring occasionally.
6. Roast thighs for 20 to 30 minutes, basting frequently with the sauce, until skin is crisp and sticky and the turkey "ribs" are fully cooked. Serve with lots of napkins.

Serves 4 to 6

Butterflied Quail with Hoisin Honey BBQ Baste

Ask your butcher to butterfly and bone the quail. This will save you a lot of time and fuss. To bone the quail on your own, cut along each side of the back bone with poultry shears. Remove the bone and splay the quail out, skin side down. Using a boning knife, carefully remove the breast bone and rib cage. Make an incision along the bone of each thigh, carefully cut around the thigh bone and remove it. Just like that, you have a boned quail.

8 quail, butterflied and mostly boneless

2 tbsp. Bone Dust BBQ Spice (see page 42)

2 green onions, minced

2 cloves garlic, minced

1/4 cup soy sauce

1/4 cup rice vinegar

2 tbsp. olive oil

1 tsp. minced fresh ginger

Hoisin Honey BBQ Baste

1/2 cup hoisin sauce

2 tbsp. honey

2 tbsp. ketchup

2 tsp. toasted sesame seeds

1 tsp. rice vinegar

Salt and cracked black pepper to taste

1. Lay quail, skin side down, on a work surface. Skewer quail in an X pattern, running two skewers across the quail from leg to breast. Rub the quail with the Bone Dust BBQ Spice. Lay the quail in a dish large enough to hold them in one layer.

2. In a bowl, stir together the green onions, garlic, soy sauce, vinegar, oil and ginger. Pour marinade over quail, turning to coat. Marinate, covered and refrigerated, for 2 hours, turning occasionally.

3. Meanwhile, make the Hoisin Honey BBQ Baste. In a bowl, stir together the hoisin sauce, honey, ketchup, sesame seeds, vinegar, salt and pepper.

4. Preheat broiler. Remove quail from marinade, discarding marinade. Place quail skin side up on a broiler pan or baking pan. Broil 2 to 3 inches below the heat for 3 to 5 minutes, until the skin begins to get crisp and golden. Turn and broil for 2 to 3 more minutes, basting with the Hoisin Honey BBQ Baste. Remove from oven and baste the skin side of the quail.

5. Serve immediately with fried rice.

Serves 4

Smoky Salt-Crusted Cornish Game Hen with Rosemary

Chef Mike McColl made this for me one day. It was based on something he learned while apprenticing in Europe. It's absolutely delicious! Leftovers make an awesome sandwich or a fabulous filling for an omelette or topping on a pizza.

6 lb. coarse kosher salt (yes, it's a lot, but you'll need it)
1/3 cup Bone Dust BBQ Spice (see page 42)
1 1/2 cups lager
2 Cornish game hens (each 1 1/2 to 2 lb.)
1/4 cup fresh rosemary leaves

1. Preheat oven to 425°F.
2. In a bowl, stir together the salt, Bone Dust BBQ Spice and beer. Set aside.
3. Remove giblets from hens and wash hens under cold water. Pat dry inside and out with paper towels. Put half of the rosemary inside each hen.
4. Spread one third of the salt mixture in a large casserole dish or roasting pan, pressing to lightly pack. Place hens, breast side down, into the salt. Top with the remaining salt mixture, packing the salt tightly around the birds to make two mounds like camel humps.
5. Roast the hens for 75 minutes. Remove from oven and let rest about 10 minutes.
6. Crack the salt crust with the back of a knife. Carefully peel off the salt crust, a little at a time. Remove hens from salt. Slice hens in half and serve. No sauce required—it's delicious as is.

Serves 4

Roast Guinea Hen with Cranberry Ice Wine Sauce

My folks used to live in the country. Our neighbours ran a farm, and for some bizarre reason their flock of guinea fowl used to love to hang out with my folks. Maybe the birds just knew that it was a guinea fowl safe zone. That is, until I came to visit …

1/4 cup + 2 tbsp. butter, softened

1 tbsp. + 1 tsp. Bone Dust BBQ Spice (see page 42)

1 guinea hen (2 1/2 to 3 1/2 lb.)

2 cloves garlic

2 sprigs thyme

3 shallots

4 slices bacon

Special equipment: a Cajun injector (or a large syringe for injecting meat)

Cranberry Ice Wine Sauce

1/2 cup dried cranberries

1 tsp. butter

1 tbsp. chopped fresh shallot

1 tsp. chopped fresh thyme

1/2 cup ice wine

2 tbsp. sugar

2 tsp. fresh lemon juice

Salt and pepper

1. In a small saucepan, melt 1/4 cup of the butter over low heat. Stir in 1 tsp. of the Bone Dust BBQ Spice. Using a Cajun injector, suck up about half of the butter. Inject the butter mixture into several places in each breast of the guinea hen. Rub the inside and outside of the guinea hen with the remaining melted butter. Rub hen with the remaining 1 tbsp. of Bone Dust, pressing the spices so they adhere. Put garlic, thyme and shallots into the cavity of the guinea hen. Transfer hen to a shallow dish and refrigerate, covered, about 30 minutes to allow the butter to harden.

2. Preheat oven to 350°F.

3. Place the guinea hen, breast side down, on a rack in a roasting pan. Lay bacon slices over the hen. Roast hen for 30 minutes. Remove bacon, turn hen breast side up, lay bacon over breast and roast for another 50 to 60 minutes, basting with the pan juices, until hen is fully cooked but still juicy. Let rest for 5 minutes.

4. While the hen is roasting, prepare the sauce. Soak the cranberries in warm water for 15 minutes; drain. In a medium saucepan over medium-high heat, melt the butter. Sauté the shallots and thyme for 1 to 2 minutes or until shallots are tender. Stir in the cranberries, ice wine and sugar. Bring to a boil. Add the lemon juice. Season to taste with salt and pepper. Reduce heat to low and simmer for 10 minutes, until thick. Set aside, keeping warm.

5. Carve the legs from the hen and cut each leg into a thigh and a drumstick. Carve the breast meat. Serve with the Cranberry Ice Wine Sauce.

Serves 2

*@µ¿?€‰! Good Lacquered Duck

If you've never had duck, then this is the best introduction. If you're familiar with this delicious bird, then this is a great way to renew your acquaintance. It has everything you want … crispy skin and well-prepared flesh. Even Daffy would approve.

1 duck (4 to 5 lb.)
Juice of 3 oranges (about 1 1/2 cups)
1/2 cup soy sauce
1/4 cup brown sugar
1 tbsp. Bone Dust BBQ Spice (see page 42)
1 tsp. salt
Salt and pepper

Grand Marnier Lacquer
1/2 cup honey
2 tbsp. Grand Marnier
Zest of 2 oranges
2 tbsp. butter

1. Ask your butcher to butterfly the duck by removing the back bone. Rinse the duck with cold water and pat dry with paper towels. Place the duck in a roasting pan.
2. In a bowl, stir together the orange juice, soy sauce, sugar, Bone Dust BBQ Spice and salt until the sugar has dissolved. Pour over the duck, turning to coat. Marinate, covered and refrigerated, for 6 to 8 hours or overnight, turning the duck several times.
3. Preheat oven to 325°F.
4. Remove duck from marinade; drain marinade into a small saucepan. Season duck with salt and pepper to taste. Place duck, skin side up, on a rack in the roasting pan. Pour 1/2 cup of the marinade and 1/2 cup water into the roasting pan.
5. To make the glaze, to the remaining marinade add the honey, Grand Marnier and orange zest. Bring to a boil over high heat. Reduce heat and simmer, stirring occasionally, until liquid is reduced by half, about 10 minutes. Remove from heat and stir in the butter until melted.
6. Roast duck for 1 1/2 hours, basting every 15 minutes with the Grand Marnier Lacquer. Increase temperature to 425°F and roast the duck for 10 to 15 minutes, glazing liberally with lacquer, until the skin is sticky sweet and crisp with a rich glaze.
7. Cut duck in half or into quarters and serve.

Serves 2 to 4

The HHH Roasted Foie Gras
with Peach, Shallot and Bourbon Relish

This foie gras is so HEAVENLY that you're sure to end up in HELL once you've had your HEART ATTACK.

3 ripe peaches

4 medium-large shallots, peeled and halved

2 tbsp. olive oil

Salt and pepper

2 tbsp. bourbon

2 tbsp. water

1 tbsp. honey

1 tsp. lemon juice

1 tbsp. chopped fresh thyme

1 lobe foie gras (1 to 1 1/2 lb.)

2 tbsp. Bone Dust BBQ Spice (see page 42)

6 to 8 slices pancetta

1 handful arugula leaves

1 handful torn frisée

1 handful torn radicchio

1/2 cup onion sprouts

Dash olive oil

Dash balsamic vinegar

1. Preheat oven to 425°F.
2. Halve and pit the peaches. In a bowl, combine the peaches, shallots, oil, salt and pepper. Stir to coat peaches well. Place peaches, cut side up, in a small roasting pan or oven-proof frying pan. Roast for 20 to 30 minutes, until tender and golden brown. Let cool slightly. Peel peaches and cut each half into three or four wedges. Slice the shallots.
3. In a small saucepan, combine the bourbon, water, honey and lemon juice. Bring to a low boil over medium heat. Stir in the thyme, roasted peaches and shallots. Season to taste with salt and pepper. Set aside.

4. Season the foie gras with Bone Dust BBQ Spice, rubbing the spices into the liver. Place in a roasting pan. Roast for 45 minutes or until golden and just firm to the touch but not rock hard. Let rest for 5 minutes.

5. Towards the end of the roasting time, gently reheat the sauce. Fry the pancetta in a small frying pan over medium-high heat until crisp. Set aside.

6. In a large bowl, combine the arugula, frisée, radicchio and onion sprouts. Sprinkle with olive oil and balsamic vinegar. Season to taste with salt and pepper. Toss well.

7. Slice foie gras into 1/2-inch-thick slices. Place a mound of the greens on each plate. Top with a slice of foie gras. Top with a slice of fried pancetta. Spoon over the warmed Peach, Shallot and Bourbon Relish and serve.

Serves 6 to 8

Wet and wild
seafood

Lobster Thermidor

This recipe calls for Taleggio, a rich cow's milk cheese from Italy's Lombardy region. If you can't find Taleggio, substitute Brie.

3 tbsp. sea salt	1/4 cup dry sherry
3 live lobsters (each 2 to 2 1/2 lb.)	2 cups Really Good Béchamel Sauce (see page 74)
2 tbsp. butter	1 cup cubed Taleggio cheese
2 cloves garlic, minced	Salt and pepper
1 jalapeño pepper, seeded and finely diced	1/2 cup seasoned dry bread crumbs
1/4 cup chopped shallots	1/4 cup grated Parmesan cheese
1 tbsp. chopped fresh thyme	1 tbsp. chopped fresh parsley
1 yellow bell pepper, roasted, seeded and diced	

1. Fill a large pot with enough water to cover the lobsters; bring to a boil. Add the sea salt. Plunge lobsters head first into the water; return to a boil. Boil lobsters for 8 minutes. Remove lobsters from water and let stand until cool enough to touch.
2. Preheat oven to 425°F.
3. Using a large, very sharp knife, slice the lobsters from head to tail down the middle. Crack open the claws. Remove the meat from the tails, claws and knuckles. Cut the meat into 1-inch chunks and transfer to a bowl. Reserve four half-shells once all the meat has been removed; discard the remaining shells.
4. In a frying pan over medium-high heat, melt the butter. Sauté the garlic, jalapeño, shallots and thyme until shallots are tender. Stir in the yellow pepper and sherry. Bring to a boil and reduce liquid, stirring occasionally, by half. Pour over lobster meat.
5. Add the béchamel and Taleggio; stir until well blended. Season to taste with salt and pepper. Spoon lobster mixture into the lobster shells, pressing firmly and packing 'em high. Place on a baking sheet.
6. Stir together the bread crumbs, Parmesan and parsley. Sprinkle the mixture over the lobster filling. Bake for 20 minutes or until heated through and the top is golden brown and crispy.
7. Serve immediately.

Serves 4

Kung Pao Shrimp with Asparagus

This recipe is a prime example of real Canadian Chinese food: you just gotta love it. Some of my favourite dishes are from restaurants like the Goof and the Moon Palace in Toronto, and The Palm in my hometown of Paris, Ontario.

1 lb. extra-large shrimp (16–20/lb. count), peeled and deveined

1/4 cup orange juice

1/4 cup rice vinegar

1 tbsp. brown sugar

1 tbsp. soy sauce

2 tsp. tapioca starch

3 tbsp. vegetable oil

1 tbsp. Bone Dust BBQ Spice (see page 42)

1 tsp. sesame oil

4 cloves garlic, minced

1 medium onion, cut into 1-inch pieces

4 to 6 dried red chilies, crushed

1 tbsp. minced fresh ginger

1 medium red bell pepper, cut into 1-inch cubes

1/2 lb. asparagus, cut into 1-inch pieces

1/2 cup cashews

1. Rinse the shrimp in cold water. Pat dry with paper towels and set aside.
2. In a large bowl, combine the orange juice, vinegar, sugar, soy sauce and tapioca starch. Whisk until starch is dissolved. Set aside.
3. In a wok or large frying pan, heat the oil over high heat. Sprinkle the shrimp with the Bone Dust BBQ Spice. Stir-fry shrimp for 2 to 3 minutes, stirring until just cooked and opaque. Remove shrimp and set aside.
4. Add sesame oil to wok. Stir-fry the garlic, onion, chilies and ginger until onions are just tender. Add red pepper, asparagus and shrimp. Whisk sauce again, add to wok and bring to the boil, stirring. Stir in the cashews.
5. Serve over rice.

Serves 4

Hot and Spicy Pan-Fried Jack Daniel's BBQ Shrimp

I had a dish similar to this at Emeril's restaurant, Nola, in New Orleans. It's an awesome dish.

1 lb. jumbo shrimp (12–15/lb. count), peeled and deveined, tails left on

2 tbsp. Bayou Bite Cajun Rub (see page 44)

2 tbsp. olive oil

4 tbsp. butter

4 cloves garlic, minced

1 hot red chili, minced

2 tbsp. Jack Daniel's

1/4 cup gourmet BBQ sauce

2 tsp. Louisiana-style hot sauce

Squeeze lemon juice

1. Rinse the shrimp in cold water. Pat dry with paper towels and put in a bowl. Add Bayou Bite Cajun Rub and toss to evenly coat. Set aside.

2. In a large frying pan (not nonstick), heat the oil and 2 tbsp. of the butter over high heat until the butter is bubbling. Add shrimp and fry, without turning, for 1 to 2 minutes or until golden brown on one side. Turn shrimp and add the garlic and chili. Stir-fry for 1 to 2 minutes, until the shrimp just turn pink. Carefully add the Jack Daniel's and light with a kitchen match. (Keep your hair out of the way!) Let cook until the flames die down.

3. Add the BBQ sauce, hot sauce, lemon juice and remaining 2 tbsp. butter; stir until heated through and the butter has melted.

4. Serve immediately over rice.

Serves 4

Coquilles St. Popeye

Coquilles St. Jacques is traditionally served in a scallop shell surrounded by mashed potatoes. My version substitutes mashed potatoes with potato chips and uses lots of spinach and crab meat.

1 lb. spinach	Pinch grated nutmeg
5 tbsp. butter	Salt and pepper to taste
1 small onion, diced	18 large sea scallops (10–20/lb. count)
3 cloves minced garlic	2 tbsp. vegetable oil
1/4 cup dry white wine	1 cup coarsely crushed potato chips
1 cup Really Good Béchamel Sauce (see page 74)	1 cup shredded Swiss cheese
1/2 cup heavy cream	1/4 cup grated Parmesan cheese
1/4 cup crumbled cream cheese	6 large scallop shells
1 1/2 cups crab meat	

1. Remove stems from the spinach leaves. Wash the leaves well in a sink full of water. Drain well.
2. In a large frying pan, melt 3 tbsp. of the butter over high heat. Sauté the onion and garlic for 2 to 3 minutes, until onions are transparent and tender. Stir in the spinach and wine. Cook until liquid is reduced by half.
3. Stir in the béchamel, cream and cream cheese. Bring to a slow boil, stirring until cream cheese is melted. Reduce heat to a simmer and cook, stirring, until sauce is thick and creamy, 1 to 2 minutes. Remove from heat and let cool slightly. Stir in the crab meat, nutmeg, salt and pepper. Let cool completely.
4. Pat the scallops dry with a paper towel. Season with salt and pepper.
5. In a medium frying pan over high heat, melt the remaining 2 tbsp. butter in the oil until the butter begins to sizzle. Working in batches if necessary so you don't crowd the pan, sear the scallops for 20 to 30 seconds per side, until lightly browned but still rare in the centre. Drain on paper towels and set aside to cool.
6. Preheat oven to 425°F.
7. Spread an even layer of coarse salt on a baking sheet and set six large scallop shells into the salt. (The salt helps keep the shells from tipping. You can also use crumpled foil. Omit the salt if you're using ramekins.) Spread a good dollop of the crab sauce in each shell. Top each with three scallops. Top the scallops with an even larger dollop of crab sauce, spreading it to cover the scallops.
8. In a bowl, stir together the potato chips, Swiss cheese and Parmesan cheese. Sprinkle evenly over each serving. (Scallops can be prepared to this point and refrigerated, covered, until needed.)
9. Bake for 10 to 15 minutes, or until heated through, bubbling, golden brown and crisp.

Serves 6

Roasted Cedar-Planked Salmon with Brown Sugar and Spice Rub and Wild Blueberry Butter Sauce

While on the island of Fogo, off the north coast of Newfoundland, I had a pan-seared salmon that was served with a wild blueberry sauce. I thought that this would make a great plank recipe, so here's my version.

3 cups cranberry or apple juice

2 cloves garlic, minced

1/4 cup light brown sugar

3 tbsp. Amazing Steak Spice (see page 43)

1 tbsp. chopped fresh thyme

4 skinless Atlantic salmon fillets (each 6 oz.)

Special equipment: 1 untreated cedar plank (at least 8 × 12 inches and 1 inch thick)

Wild Blueberry Butter Sauce

4 tbsp. cold butter

2 shallots, finely chopped

1 cup fresh wild blueberries

1/4 cup Riesling

1 tsp. chopped fresh thyme

Pinch cinnamon

Salt and freshly ground black pepper

1. Preheat oven to 450°F.
2. Place the plank in a deep baking pan large enough to hold it. Pour the cranberry juice around the plank until it floats. Heat plank in oven for 10 minutes or until you can smell the cedar. Remove the plank from the pan.
3. Meanwhile, in a small bowl, stir together the garlic, sugar, steak spice and thyme. Rub the spice mixture all over the salmon, pressing firmly so the spices adhere.
4. Place the salmon on the plank. Return the plank to the baking pan and bake for 15 to 20 minutes for medium to medium-well. Keep an eye on the liquid, and add more juice or water if the pan looks dry.
5. While the salmon is planking, prepare the Wild Blueberry Butter Sauce. In a small saucepan, melt 1 tbsp. of the butter over medium heat. Add the shallots; cook for 1 to 2 minutes or until transparent

and tender. Add the blueberries and cook, stirring, for 2 to 4 minutes, until the blueberries start to split open. Stir in the wine. Cook, stirring, until the liquid is reduced by one quarter. Stir in the thyme. Remove from heat and stir in the remaining 3 tbsp. of butter 1 tbsp. at a time, stirring until butter is melted before adding more. Season to taste with cinnamon, salt and pepper.

6. Using a spatula, transfer the salmon to plates. Spoon 2 or 3 tbsp. of blueberry sauce over the fish. Serve immediately.

Serves 4

Note: Fogo (the word means "fire" in Portuguese) Island is the northwest corner of the "flat earth society." If you are ever in Newfoundland, Fogo is a must-see island. Check out the F. U. Trading Company (that stands for Fishermen's Union, by the way). It provides a great deal of history about the island of Fogo.

Cedar-Planked Cod with Coldwater Shrimp, Scrunchions and Black Horse Ale Butter Sauce

If you can't find Newfoundland's Black Horse Ale, substitute your favourite ale.

4 boneless skinless fresh cod loins (each 6 oz. and
    1 to 1 1/2 inches thick)

2 bottles Black Horse Ale

1 tbsp. Bone Dust BBQ Spice (see page 42)

1 tbsp. chopped fresh savory (or 2 tsp. dried)

1/2 cup diced salt pork

1 medium Yukon Gold potato, diced

1 green onion, chopped

1 cup cooked baby shrimp

1/4 cup finely diced red onion

1/4 cup cold butter

Salt and pepper

Special equipment: 1 untreated cedar plank (at least
    8 × 10 inches and 1/2 inch thick), soaked in cold
    water for at least 1 hour

1. Place the cod loins in a glass dish large enough to hold them in one layer. Pour one bottle of the Black Horse Ale over the cod. Marinate cod at room temperature for 30 minutes.

2. Meanwhile, preheat oven to 425°F.

3. Reserve 1/4 cup of the marinade. Drain cod (discarding remaining marinade) and pat dry with paper towels. Stir together the Bone Dust BBQ Spice and savory. Rub the mixture all over the cod loins to evenly coat.

4. Place the plank in a deep baking pan large enough to hold it. Pour the second bottle of ale into the pan, then add water until the plank floats. Heat plank in oven for 10 minutes or until you can smell the cedar.

5. Arrange the cod loins on the plank. Bake for 15 to 18 minutes or until just cooked through. Keep an eye on the liquid, and add more ale or water if the pan looks dry.

6. While the cod is planking, prepare the sauce. In a medium frying pan over medium-high heat, fry the salt pork, stirring, until crisp, 3 to 5 minutes. Using a slotted spoon, remove the scrunchions from the pan and set aside. Fry the potatoes in the fat in the pan, stirring constantly, until crispy, golden and tender, about 5 minutes. Stir in the green onion, shrimp, red onion and reserved marinade. Bring to a boil. Remove from heat. Add the butter and scrunchions; stir until butter is melted. Season to taste with salt and pepper.

7. Transfer the fish to plates and dust with salt. Serve with the sauce.

Serves 4

Granite Grouper with Mangoes and Orange Butter

Cooking on granite provides a hot, even baking surface, helping to sear and seal in the juices of a variety of foods. You can find granite slabs in specialty home shops.

1/2 cup orange juice or mango juice

Zest of 1 orange

1/4 cup chopped green onions

2 tbsp. olive oil

1 tbsp. chopped fresh thyme

1 tbsp. chopped fresh ginger

1 tbsp. sea salt

1 tsp. cracked black pepper

4 skinless grouper fillets (each 6 to 8 oz. and 1 1/2 inches thick)

1 large firm mango, peeled and thinly sliced

1/4 cup butter

Special equipment: 1 smooth granite slab (at least 8 × 10 inches and 1 inch thick)

1. In a large bowl, stir together the orange juice, orange zest, green onions, 1 tbsp. of the oil, the thyme, ginger, salt and pepper. Submerse the grouper in the juice mixture, turning to coat, and marinate, covered and refrigerated, for 20 minutes.

2. Meanwhile, preheat oven to 450°F.

3. Place granite on the middle shelf of oven and heat for 15 minutes. Brush the granite with the remaining oil. Arrange the mango slices, overlapping, down the centre of the granite to make a bed slightly larger than the fish. Remove the grouper from marinade (reserving marinade) and arrange over the mango slices. Bake for 12 to 15 minutes or until fish is just cooked through and flakes with a fork.

4. In a small saucepan, bring the marinade to a boil over high heat. Remove from heat. Add the butter; stir until the butter has melted.

5. Arrange grouper fillets and some mango slices on four plates. Drizzle with the orange sauce and serve immediately.

Serves 4

Paper-Wrapped Pickerel with Sweet and Smoky Herb Butter

This dish may sound unusual because it calls for pine shavings, but trust me, they add a great flavour. (You can also use maple, oak or Western red cedar.) Just be careful not to eat the shavings.

1 piece untreated pine (a 12-inch piece of 2 × 4 is perfect)

2 medium leeks (white and pale green part only)

8 tbsp. butter

1/4 cup chopped shallots

1 tbsp. freshly grated ginger

Zest and juice of 1 lime

2 tbsp. chopped fresh chives

Salt and pepper

6 skinless fresh pickerel or salmon fillets (each 6 oz.)

1/2 cup sake

1. Set the piece of pine in a vise. Using a hand-held planer, plane 12 wafer-thin shavings from the pine.
2. Cut the leeks in half lengthwise. Rinse under cold water to remove all grit. Drain well. Cut leeks diagonally into 1/2-inch pieces.
3. Melt 2 tbsp. of the butter in a medium frying pan over medium-high heat. Sauté the leeks for 2 to 3 minutes, until they just begin to wilt. Add the shallots and ginger; sauté for another 2 minutes. Remove from heat. Stir in the lime zest and juice; let cool. Stir in the chives, salt and pepper.
4. Preheat oven to 425°F.
5. Cut six squares of parchment paper about 20 inches long and fold a crease down the middle so you have two 10-inch halves. Place two pine shavings on one half of each sheet.
6. Season the pickerel to taste with salt and pepper. Place pickerel, skinned side down, on top of the pine shavings. Top with the leek mixture. Drizzle each with 1 tbsp. of the sake and top with 1 tbsp. of the remaining butter. Fold the paper over the pickerel. Starting at one corner, fold over and crimp the edges of the paper to form a sealed packet. When you reach the end, tuck the last fold underneath the packet to secure. Transfer packets to a baking sheet.
7. Bake for 20 minutes, until fish is fully cooked and firm to the touch. Transfer the packets to plates and let people cut them open at the table to enjoy the aromas.

Serves 6

Striped Bass Baked in Salt Crust

I first had fish baked in a salt crust when I was in Turkey on a world spice tour with chefs and food writers. The salt-crusted fish was one of the highlights of the trip.

4 1/2 lb. coarse kosher salt

1/4 cup Bone Dust BBQ Spice (see page 42)

1 cup lager

Juice of 1 lime

4 green onions, chopped

2 tbsp. chopped fresh parsley

1 tbsp. chopped fresh chives

1 tbsp. chopped fresh thyme

2 striped bass (each 1 1/2 to 2 lb.), dressed and scaled, heads left on but tails removed

Lime wedges, for garnish

1. Preheat oven to 425°F.
2. In a large bowl, stir together the salt, Bone Dust BBQ Spice and beer.
3. In another bowl, stir together the lime juice, green onions, parsley, chives and thyme. Stuff the bass with the herb mixture.
4. Spread half the salt mixture evenly in a 10 × 16-inch baking sheet. Lay the stuffed fish down the length of the baking sheet. Pour the rest of the salt mixture over the fish. Pack the salt tightly over the top and sides of the fish to completely encrust. Bake for 30 minutes. Remove from oven and let the fish rest for 5 minutes.
5. With the back of a knife, crack open the salt crust and carefully peel off the crust to expose the bass. Peel the skin from the top of the bass. Using a knife, gently remove the top two fillets and transfer to serving plates. Carefully turn fish and repeat. Repeat with remaining fish. Serve with lime wedges.

Serves 4

Confit of Sea Bass with Tangy Champagne Orange Drizzling

A confit is a classic French method of preserving meats in goose or duck fat. Chefs are always striving to change the classic. My sea bass is lightly seasoned and then slowly poached in duck fat. It is extremely rich but delicately delicious. For those of you who love sea bass, this recipe is truly to die for.

4 skinless sea bass fillets (each about 6 oz. and 1 1/2 inches thick)

1 tbsp. cracked black pepper

Sea salt to taste

3 seedless oranges

2 tbsp. cold butter

1/4 cup chopped shallots

1 tsp. minced fresh ginger

1/4 cup champagne

1/4 cup fresh orange juice

2 tsp. tapioca starch or cornstarch, dissolved in a little water

1 tbsp. chopped fresh lemon thyme

1. In a large saucepan, melt the duck fat over medium heat. Carefully strain fat through a fine-mesh strainer to remove bits of skin. Return fat to pan and set aside.
2. Pat sea bass dry with paper towels. Rub with black pepper and sea salt. Set aside.
3. Using a sharp knife, cut the rind and white pith from the oranges. Using a sharp paring knife and working over a bowl to catch the juices, cut between the membranes to remove the segments. Set aside.
4. In a small saucepan over medium-high heat, melt the butter. Sauté the shallots and ginger for 1 to 2 minutes, until shallots are transparent and tender. Add the champagne and orange juice. Bring to a boil, reduce heat and simmer until reduced by one third.
5. Stir in the dissolved tapioca starch and return to a boil. Cook, stirring, until thick. Remove from heat and stir in orange segments and thyme. Season to taste with salt and pepper. Set aside, keeping warm.
6. Heat the duck fat to 225°F. Gently slip the seasoned bass into the fat. Cook for 10 to 15 minutes, until just cooked through, tender and flaky. Gently remove bass and drain on paper towels.
7. Transfer bass to plates, spoon orange sauce over bass and serve immediately.

Serves 4

Pepper Tuna Steaks with Wasabi Butter

Ah wa-sa-bi. The Japanese horseradish is sometimes known as the nasal buster. It's sharp, hot and pungent! Blending it with butter smooths it out and enriches the tuna. This dish goes great with a salad and Lemon Soy Vinaigrette (see page 94).

2 tbsp. wasabi powder

1/2 cup butter, softened

2 tbsp. finely chopped chives

2 tbsp. pineapple juice

Coarse salt to taste

4 tuna steaks (each 8 oz. and 1 1/2 inches thick)

1/4 cup Amazing Steak Spice (see page 43)

1/4 cup vegetable oil

1. In a small bowl, add a drizzle of water to the wasabi powder and stir until it forms a smooth, thick paste. In a bowl, combine the wasabi paste, butter, chives, pineapple juice and salt; beat until smooth. Transfer to a sheet of wax paper, and using the wax paper as a guide, shape it into a log about 2 inches thick and 6 inches long. Refrigerate the butter, wrapped in the wax paper, until firm.
2. Season the tuna steaks with the steak spice, pressing the spice firmly but gently into the fish so it adheres.
3. In a large frying pan, heat the oil over medium-high heat. Sear the tuna steaks for 2 to 3 minutes per side. Do not overcook. The tuna is ready when the centre is slightly warm but still raw.
4. Transfer tuna to plates and top each steak with 1 tbsp. of wasabi butter. Serve immediately.

Serves 4

St. Lucia Mahi Mahi in a Creole Quick Braise

While we were working on this book in St. Lucia, our driver took us out of town to find some fish. At a fish stand at the side of the road, we purchased amazingly fresh mahi mahi. It was fantastic! Firm-fleshed mahi is perfect for the grill.

4 skinless mahi mahi fillets (each 8 oz.)
2 tbsp. Bayou Bite Cajun Rub (see page 44)
2 tbsp. butter
1 medium red bell pepper, sliced
1 medium green bell pepper, sliced
1 medium onion, sliced
2 cups okra, stems removed and sliced in half lengthwise
1/4 cup lager
2 cups Really Good Tomato Sauce (see page 73)
1 tbsp. sugar
2 tbsp. chopped fresh cilantro
Squeeze fresh lime juice

1. Season the mahi mahi with 1 tbsp. of the Cajun Rub, gently pressing the spices into the fish.
2. In a large frying pan over high heat, melt the butter. Sear the mahi mahi, about 2 minutes per side. Remove the fish from the pan and set aside.
3. In the same pan over medium heat, stir-fry the peppers and onion for 4 to 5 minutes, until browned and softened. Add the okra; cook for 3 minutes, stirring frequently. Stir in the beer, tomato sauce and sugar. Place the fish on top of the vegetables, reduce heat to medium-low and cover. Cook the mahi mahi for 5 minutes or until fish is cooked through.
4. Serve immediately, garnished with cilantro and a squeeze of lime.

Serves 4

Blackened Snapper with Baby Shrimp and Herb Butter

I like to do this snapper outside, on the side burner of my grill. It's best done in the great outdoors 'cuz then it doesn't fill the house with stinky smoke. If you have to do it indoors, make sure you have great ventilation in your kitchen.

1/4 cup Bayou Bite Cajun Rub (see page 44)

2 tbsp. butter, softened

4 red snapper fillets (each 6 to 8 oz.)

1 tbsp. olive oil

1 lb. baby shrimp

1 large red bell pepper, diced

1/4 cup dry white wine

Juice of 1 lemon

Juice of 1 lime

3 green onions, chopped

3 tbsp. cold butter

1. Preheat oven to 350°F. Line a baking sheet with foil.
2. Blend together the Cajun Rub and softened butter until smooth. Using your hands, smear the butter onto both sides of the fish.
3. In a well-ventilated kitchen, heat a large, heavy dry frying pan over high heat until just smoking. Cook fish for 1 to 3 minutes per side, until golden brown. There will be a fair amount of smoke! Transfer fish to the baking sheet and keep warm in the oven.
4. In the same pan over medium heat, heat the olive oil. Cook the shrimp and red pepper for 2 minutes. Add the wine, lemon juice, lime juice and green onions. Cook for 3 minutes or until the liquid has reduced by half. Remove from heat, add the cold butter, and stir until the butter is incorporated.
5. Place the blackened snapper on plates. Pour the baby shrimp butter over the fish and serve immediately.

Serves 4

Cajun Salmon Stir-Fry

I like to make this quick and healthful stir-fry with farm-raised Heritage-brand Atlantic salmon. It's the best salmon, homegrown in Canada. But any salmon will do just fine.

2 skinless salmon fillets (each about 5 oz.)

1/4 cup + 2 tbsp. vegetable oil

1 tbsp. Bayou Bite Cajun Rub (see page 44)

1 clove garlic, minced

1/2 small red onion, sliced

1 tsp. minced fresh ginger

1 small yellow bell pepper, thinly sliced

1 cup sugar snap peas OR 8 spears asparagus, cut into 1-inch lengths

1/4 cup beer

1/4 cup ketchup

2 tbsp. butter

2 tbsp. honey

1 tbsp. chopped fresh cilantro

1 tbsp. Louisiana-style hot sauce

1 tbsp. lemon juice

Salt

1. Place salmon on a plate and freeze for 15 minutes. (Really cold fish is easier to slice evenly.) Using a sharp knife, slice the salmon into 1/2-inch-thick strips. Place in a bowl and add 2 tbsp. of the oil and the Cajun Rub. Combine thoroughly. Marinate salmon, covered and refrigerated, for 1 hour.

2. Heat a wok or large nonstick frying pan over high heat until the pan begins to smoke. Add the remaining 1/4 cup of oil. Add the salmon; stir-fry, stirring gently, until seared. Gently remove from pan and set aside.

3. In the same pan, stir-fry the garlic, onions and ginger for 1 minute or until onions are just tender. Add the yellow pepper and peas; stir-fry until the peas are bright green, 1 to 2 minutes. Return salmon to the wok and gently stir. Add beer, ketchup, butter, honey, cilantro, hot sauce and lemon juice. Bring to a boil; boil for 1 minute or until sauce is thick. Season to taste with salt.

4. Serve with fried rice.

Serves 2

Pan-Fried Trout with Roasted Yellow Pepper, Peach and Saffron Broth

I'm a big fan of trout. I remember trout fishing in Northern Ontario with my brother Edward. He is not a fisherman but more of a lie-down-in-the-boat-and-sleep kind of guy. I fished, he slept. I cooked. The trout was stellar.

2 large yellow bell peppers	Good pinch saffron
6 tbsp. butter	2 cups Really Good Fish Stock (see page 72)
2 shallots, diced	3 ripe peaches, peeled and cut into 1/2-inch wedges
1 red hot chili, finely chopped	1 small leek, cleaned well and sliced
1 tsp. minced fresh ginger	1 tbsp. chopped fresh cilantro
2 tbsp. all-purpose flour	Salt and pepper
1/4 cup dry white wine	3 tbsp. olive oil
1 tbsp. lemon juice	4 rainbow trout fillets (each about 5 oz.)

1. Preheat oven to 425°F.
2. Roast yellow peppers directly on the oven rack until the skin is black and blistered, about 45 minutes. Transfer peppers to a bowl and cover with plastic wrap. Let stand 15 minutes. Peel and seed peppers. Cut into 1/2-inch pieces and set aside.
3. In a medium frying pan, melt 2 tbsp. of the butter over medium-high heat. Add the shallots, chili and ginger; sauté for 1 to 2 minutes or until shallots are tender. Sprinkle with the flour and stir. Stir in the roasted peppers, wine, lemon juice and saffron; cook, stirring, until the sauce bubbles. Stir in the fish stock, a little at a time; bring to a boil. Stir in the peaches and leeks. Reduce heat to low, cover and simmer for 10 minutes or until peaches and leeks are tender. Stir in 2 tbsp. of the butter until melted. Stir in the cilantro, and salt and pepper to taste. Set aside and keep warm.
4. Heat the oil and remaining 2 tbsp. butter in a large frying pan over medium-high heat. Add the trout, skin side down, and fry for about 2 minutes, until skin is lightly browned. Turn and fry for 1 minute more or until the fish is cooked through and lightly browned.
5. Spoon the broth into pasta or soup plates. Top with the trout and serve immediately.

Serves 4

Fogo Island Seafood Casserole

Fogo Island is a thirty-minute ferry ride off the north coast of Newfoundland. It's home to a seafood company called the Fogo Co-op, or at one time, the F. U. (Fishermen's Union) Trading Company.

1 lb. medium scallops

1 lb. jumbo shrimp (11–15/lb. count)

1/2 lb. skinless white fish fillets (such as halibut, sea bass or cod), cut into 1 1/2-inch cubes

1/2 lb. skinless salmon fillets, cut into 1 1/2-inch cubes

2 cups cooked mussel meat (from about 1 lb. mussels, steamed)

1 tbsp. chopped fresh thyme

1 tsp. dried dill

Pinch cayenne pepper

Salt and black pepper

3 tbsp. butter

3 cloves garlic, minced

1 medium onion, diced

1 stalk celery, diced

1 medium carrot, diced

1 medium leek, diced

2 cups Really Good Béchamel Sauce (see page 74)

1 cup shredded Swiss cheese

1/2 cup white wine (such as Riesling)

2 cups Hostess Hickory Sticks

1. Preheat oven to 350°F. Grease an 8- to 10-inch 6-inch-deep casserole dish.
2. In a large bowl combine the scallops, shrimp, white fish, salmon, mussels, thyme, dill, cayenne, salt and black pepper. Stir to combine well.
3. In a large frying pan, melt the butter over high heat. Add the garlic, onion, celery, carrot and leek; sauté for 4 to 5 minutes or until tender. Add vegetables to seafood. Add the béchamel, Swiss cheese and wine. Stir until well combined. Pour into casserole dish.
4. Bake, covered, for 20 minutes. Uncover and bake for another 10 to 15 minutes or until the fish is cooked and the sauce is thick and creamy.
5. Top with Hickory Sticks and serve.

Serves 8

Tuna, Shrimp and Crab Meat Cobbler

Mom's tuna casserole this ain't. Loaded with seafood, it's gooey, creamy and cheesy. And it's delicious.

The "Cob"

2 cups Really Good Béchamel Sauce (see page 74), cooled slightly

2 cans tuna, drained

2 cups fresh crab meat

1 cup cooked baby shrimp

1 cup thawed frozen peas

1/4 cup grated Parmesan cheese

1/4 cup shredded mozzarella cheese

1 small onion, diced

1 tbsp. chopped flat-leaf parsley

Splash dry sherry

Salt and pepper

The "Bler"

1/4 cup butter

2 tbsp. Bone Dust BBQ Spice (see page 42)

1 large egg

1 cup shredded mozzarella or Cheddar cheese

1 1/2 cups all-purpose flour

2 tsp. baking powder

Pinch salt

1/2 cup table cream (18%)

1. Preheat oven to 425°F. Grease an 8-cup casserole dish.
2. To make the "Cob," in a bowl, combine the béchamel, tuna, crab meat, shrimp, peas, Parmesan, mozzarella, onion, parsley, sherry, salt and pepper. Stir well. Pour into the casserole dish.
3. To make the "Bler," in a large bowl, cream the butter. Add the Bone Dust BBQ Spice; beat until smooth. Add the egg and cheese; beat until incorporated. Sift together the flour, baking powder and salt. Add flour mixture and cream alternately to cheese mixture in three batches, mixing until smooth.
4. Pour the biscuit batter over the seafood mixture. Bake, uncovered, for 30 to 40 minutes, until topping is golden brown and set and the filling is heated through. Let cool for 10 minutes before serving.
5. Serve with mashed potatoes and ice-cold beer.

Serves 6

Swanky sides

Mashed Yucca

Yucca—a great alternative to the potato—is a long tubular root vegetable often sold in the specialty produce section of most grocery stores. A staple in Brazilian and Dominican diets, it is usually coated with wax for preserving the product, much like rutabaga.

2 lb. yucca, peeled and cut into 1 1/2-inch chunks
4 cloves garlic, chopped
2 tsp. salt
1/2 cup chicken stock
2 tbsp. butter
2 tbsp. chopped fresh chives
Salt and pepper

1. In a colander, rinse the yucca under cold running water for about 2 minutes. Place the yucca and garlic in a large pot and cover with cold water. Bring to a rolling boil over high heat. Add the salt. Reduce heat and simmer the yucca, uncovered, for 45 to 60 minutes or until it is tender. Drain, reserving 1/4 cup of the cooking water.

2. Return yucca and reserved cooking water to the pot and bring to a boil. Reduce the heat to very low, stir, and cook, covered, for 10 minutes, stirring occasionally to keep the yucca from sticking to the bottom of the pot.

3. Add the stock, butter, and chives, and salt and pepper to taste. Stir enough to lightly mash the yucca, but keep it fairly chunky.

4. Serve hot with steaks, chicken and stews.

Serves 6 to 8

And Then There Was Yucca Hash

4 slices bacon, chopped

1 medium onion, diced

4 cups white mushrooms, each cut into 8 wedges

4 cups leftover mashed yucca (see page 206)

2 tbsp. butter

1 to 2 tsp. Bone Dust BBQ Spice (see page 42)

1. In a large nonstick frying pan, fry the bacon until partly crisp. Add the onion and mushrooms; cook, stirring frequently, until they are just cooked through. Using a slotted spoon, transfer the bacon mixture to a bowl.
2. Over medium-high heat, fry the yucca in the bacon drippings for 6 to 8 minutes per side, until the yucca is golden brown, crisp on the outside and hot on the inside.
3. Remove from the heat and, using a wooden spoon, stir in the bacon mixture, butter and Bone Dust BBQ Spice to taste.
4. Serve hot with poached eggs and some ketchup or hot sauce.

Serves 8

Butter-Fried Oven-Roasted Potatoes

My grandmother made these for me when she served roast chicken. My grandfather Opi and I would eat bowls of the buttery oven-fried taters and wash 'em down with moist roast chicken and a glass of pilsner.

1/2 lb. butter

8 medium Yukon Gold potatoes, cut into 1- to 2-inch chunks

8 cloves garlic, minced

1 large sweet onion, sliced

1 tbsp. Bone Dust BBQ Spice (see page 42)

3/4 cup Really Good Chicken Stock (see page 71)

1/3 cup grated Parmesan cheese

1. Preheat oven to 400°F.
2. In a saucepan over low heat, slowly melt the butter. Cook gently so that most of the water in the butter evaporates and the milk solids sink to the bottom. Skim any foam from the surface. Carefully pour off the clear clarified butter. (You should have 3/4 cup.)
3. In a large bowl, combine the potatoes, garlic, onion, Bone Dust BBQ Spice and clarified butter. Stir to evenly coat. Spread mixture in a 13 × 9-inch baking pan. Pour in the chicken stock. Cover pan tightly with foil. Roast, stirring occasionally, until tender, 50 to 60 minutes.
4. Uncover and sprinkle with Parmesan cheese. Bake, uncovered, until cheese is bubbling and golden, 5 to 10 minutes. Serve immediately.

Serves 4 to 6

Boiled Potatoes with Pesto Butter and Parmesan

Boil 'em up tender, add lots of butter, pesto, and cheese ... and smile.

2 lb. medium Yukon Gold potatoes, peeled and cut into 1/2-inch chunks

1 tsp. salt

1/4 cup pesto (see page 92)

1/4 cup butter, softened

1/4 cup grated Parmesan cheese

1. In a large pot of cold water, bring potatoes to a rolling boil over high heat. Add salt. Boil until tender, 30 to 40 minutes. Drain potatoes. Return potatoes to the pan and shake pan over low heat until potatoes are dry.

2. Remove from heat. Gently stir in the pesto and butter. Sprinkle liberally with Parmesan cheese. Serve immediately.

Serves 4 to 6

Fully Loaded Baked Stuffed Potatoes

Bake 'em. Scoop 'em. Stuff 'em. Overstuff 'em. Bake 'em again and dig in. My favourite potato is a jumbo baker (weighing about 1 lb. each) from Idaho. A real treat when you can get them.

6 large baking potatoes (each 8 to 12 oz.)

2 tbsp. melted butter

1 tbsp. kosher salt

1 tbsp. Bone Dust BBQ Spice (see page 42), plus additional for sprinkling

1/4 cup butter, softened

1/4 cup sour cream

1/4 cup heavy cream

1/4 cup shredded yellow Cheddar cheese

2 cups shredded Swiss cheese

Salt and pepper

8 slices bacon, diced and cooked crisp

1 cup diced smoked chicken

2 green onions, chopped

1. Preheat oven to 450°F.
2. Scrub potatoes well and pat dry. In a large bowl, stir together the melted butter, salt and Bone Dust BBQ Spice. Add potatoes and turn them to evenly coat, rubbing the spice mixture over them with your hands.
3. Bake potatoes directly on the middle rack until very tender, 45 to 75 minutes. Remove from oven and let cool for 5 minutes. Reduce oven temperature to 400°F.
4. Cut potatoes in half lengthwise. Carefully scoop out the flesh, leaving a 1/2-inch-thick shell. Put 6 or 8 of the best-looking potato shells on a baking sheet. (Save remaining skins for another snack.)
5. In a large bowl, mash the potato. Add the softened butter, sour cream, heavy cream, Cheddar, 1 cup of the Swiss cheese, and salt and pepper to taste. Stir until the mixture is light and fluffy. Fold in bacon, chicken and green onions.
6. Pile potato mixture high into the 6 or 8 potato shells. Sprinkle with the remaining Swiss cheese and the Bone Dust BBQ Spice. (Potatoes can be covered and refrigerated up to 4 hours.) Bake potatoes for 15 to 20 minutes, until heated through and lightly browned.
7. Drizzle with BBQ sauce or gravy and serve immediately.

Serves 6 or 8

Scalloped Potatoes and Sweet Corn (Heaven in a Pan)

Creamy potatoes and corn topped with cheese … that's what I call heaven!

6 medium Yukon Gold potatoes

2 cups Really Good Béchamel Sauce (see page 74)

1/2 cup heavy cream

1/2 cup Really Good Chicken Stock (see page 71) or water

1/2 cup grated Parmesan cheese

2 cups fresh or thawed frozen corn kernels

2 cloves garlic, minced

1 small onion, diced

1 tbsp. chopped fresh herbs (such as thyme, marjoram and parsley)

Salt and pepper

1 cup shredded Jack cheese

1. Preheat oven to 350°F. Butter a 13 × 9-inch casserole dish.
2. Using a mandoline, thinly slice the potatoes. Place potatoes in a large bowl and rinse with cold water. Drain and cover with moist paper towel to keep from turning brown.
3. In a bowl, whisk together the béchamel, cream, stock and Parmesan until smooth.
4. In another bowl, stir together the corn, garlic, onion and herbs. Season to taste with salt and pepper.
5. Layer one third of the potatoes evenly across the bottom of the casserole, overlapping slightly. Spread with half of the corn mixture. Spread with one third of the béchamel mixture. Layer on the next third of the potatoes. Add half of the remaining corn mixture and another third of the béchamel mixture. Continue layering with the remaining potatoes, corn and béchamel mixture.
6. Cover with foil and bake for 60 minutes or until potatoes are tender. Remove foil and bake until lightly brown, about 5 minutes.
7. Remove from oven. Top with shredded cheese and let it melt. Serve immediately.

Serves 6

Lobster and Brie Mashed Potatoes

Serve this on a big plastic sheet, with bottles of champagne and the one you love. Oh yeah, baby!

3 lb. Yukon Gold potatoes, peeled

3 tbsp. butter

1/2 cup heavy cream

1 lb. cooked lobster meat, cut into 1-inch chunks

1 cup cubed Brie cheese (with rind removed)

1/4 cup chopped fresh chives

Salt and pepper

1/4 cup warm clarified butter (see page 208)

1 tbsp. very good caviar

1. In a large pot of boiling salted water, cook the potatoes until tender, 30 to 40 minutes. Drain well and return to pot over low heat for 1 minute, to dry the potatoes.
2. Mash the potatoes. Beat in the butter and cream. Stir in the lobster meat, Brie and chives. Season to taste with salt and pepper.
3. Spoon the mashed potatoes onto six plates. Drizzle with the clarified butter and top each serving with 1/2 tsp. of caviar. Serve with a bib.

Serves 2 privately or 6 for a party

Granite Grouper with Mangoes and Orange Butter (page 193)

Crème Brûlée Cheesecakes (page 232)

Stompin' Tom Mash Potatoes

Spicy, creamy, cheesy ... the best! My tribute mashed potato recipe in honor of Stompin' Tom Connors.

3 lb. Yukon Gold potatoes, peeled

3 tbsp. butter

2 medium poblano peppers, roasted, peeled, seeded and diced

1/2 cup Avocado Ranch Dressing (see page 93)

1/4 cup finely chopped fresh thyme

1/4 cup heavy cream

1 tbsp. Bone Dust BBQ Spice (see page 42)

1 cup shredded pepper Jack cheese

1 cup Poker Salsa (see page 52)

1. In a large pot of boiling salted water, cook the potatoes until tender, 30 to 40 minutes. Drain well and return pot to low heat for 1 minute, to dry the potato.
2. Mash the potatoes. Beat in the butter. Stir in the poblano peppers, ranch dressing, thyme, cream, thyme, Bone Dust BBQ Spice and 1/2 cup of the pepper Jack cheese.
3. Spoon the mashed potatoes onto six plates. Garnish with Poker Salsa and remaining pepper Jack cheese. Serve immediately.

Serves 6

Wendy's Creamed Peas

My friend Wendy makes the best creamed peas. To die for. She says this recipe is better than sex. (Or did she say it's as good as sex?)

1 lb. fresh or frozen peas

6 slices thick-cut double-smoked bacon, cut into 1/2-inch strips

3 cloves garlic, minced

1 medium onion, diced

1 small leek, washed well and thinly sliced

1 tbsp. butter

2 cups quartered button mushrooms

1 cup thawed frozen pearl onions

1/4 cup Riesling wine

1 1/2 cups Really Good Béchamel Sauce (see page 74)

1/2 cup (approx.) heavy cream

Freshly grated nutmeg, salt and pepper

1 cup thinly sliced butter lettuce

1/4 cup grated Parmesan cheese

1. If using frozen peas, thaw and drain well. If using fresh peas, blanch them in 4 cups of boiling salted water for 3 minutes, then drain and cool under cold running water to stop the cooking; drain well.
2. In a medium frying pan, fry the bacon over medium-high heat until just crisp, 5 to 10 minutes. Using a slotted spoon, transfer bacon to a bowl, reserving the fat in the pan.
3. In the same pan, fry the garlic, onion and leek in the bacon fat, stirring, until tender, 2 to 4 minutes. Add to the bacon.
4. Melt the butter in the pan and fry the mushrooms, stirring frequently, until golden brown and just crisp. Stir in the bacon, the onion mixture, the pearl onions and wine. Bring to a boil.
5. Stir in the béchamel and cream. Reduce heat to medium and bring to a low boil. Stir in the peas and a little more cream if the mixture is too thick. Season to taste with nutmeg, salt and pepper. Simmer for 15 minutes, stirring, until the mixture is thick and creamy.
6. Stir in the lettuce and Parmesan cheese. Adjust seasoning and serve immediately.

Serves 2 to 8

Cheesy Kohlrabi

My friend the Koos Koos, Chris and Karen, made this for dinner one night for my wife, Pamela, and me. It rocked! Serve it with prime rib or steaks.

8 medium kohlrabi, peeled and cut into 1/4-inch slices
1/2 tsp. salt
1 cup Really Good Béchamel Sauce (see page 74)
1/2 cup (approx.) Really Good Chicken Stock (see page 71)
1/4 cup shredded white Cheddar cheese
1/2 tsp. ground allspice
Salt and pepper
2 tbsp. chopped fresh parsley

1. Cover kohlrabi with cold water in a medium saucepan. Bring to a boil. Add salt. Reduce heat to low and simmer for about 30 minutes, until tender. Drain well.
2. In the same saucepan, stir together the béchamel and stock. Cook over medium heat, stirring, until sauce is heated through and thick. Remove from heat. Stir in the cheese until melted and smooth.
3. Add the kohlrabi and cook until heated through. Add a little more stock if the sauce is too thick. Season with allspice, and salt and pepper to taste.
4. Serve immediately, sprinkled with chopped parsley.

Serves 6

Whole Lotta Love Rum and Raisin Carrots

Why have the same old carrots? Jazz 'em up with rum, raisins and a whole lotta love, baby!

4 cups chicken stock

1/2 tsp. salt

1 lb. peeled baby carrots

1/2 cup orange marmalade

1/4 cup raisins

1/4 cup orange juice

3 tbsp. butter

2 tbsp. chopped fresh parsley

1 tbsp. lemon juice

Splash dark rum

Pinch freshly grated nutmeg

Salt and pepper

1. In a medium saucepan, bring the stock to a boil. Add the salt. Add the carrots and return to a boil. Reduce heat and simmer for 5 to 10 minutes or until carrots are just tender. Drain carrots and return to the pot.
2. Add the marmalade, raisins, orange juice, butter, parsley, lemon juice and rum. Stir over medium heat until all is melted and blended. Season with a pinch of nutmeg, and salt and pepper to taste. Serve immediately.

Serves 4 to 6

Tip: If using frozen baby carrots, skip the boiling step. Just put the frozen carrots into the pot with all the remaining ingredients and cook 'em up.

Cheesy Cauliflower

Cauliflower and cheese sauce is a classic recipe. Warms ya through and through.

1 head cauliflower, trimmed

2 cups (approx.) Really Good Chicken Stock (see page 71) or water

1 1/2 cups Really Good Béchamel Sauce (see page 74)

1 cup shredded white Cheddar cheese

1/2 cup grated Parmesan cheese

1/4 cup heavy cream

1/4 cup dry white wine

Salt and pepper

1 large hard-cooked egg, grated

1 tbsp. chopped fresh flat-leaf parsley

1. In a pot large enough to accommodate the whole cauliflower, bring the stock to a boil. Place the cauliflower in the boiling stock, cover and steam for 15 minutes or until tender.
2. Meanwhile, in a small saucepan, whisk together the béchamel, Cheddar cheese, 1/4 cup of the Parmesan cheese, the cream and wine. Stirring constantly over medium heat, heat the cheese sauce until the cheese is melted and the sauce is thick but not gluey, about 5 minutes. If it's too thick, stir in a little more stock or water. Season to taste with salt and pepper. Set aside and keep warm.
3. Carefully transfer cauliflower to a serving platter. Pour the warm cheese sauce over it. Sprinkle with remaining 1/4 cup Parmesan, the egg and parsley. Serve immediately.

Serves 6 to 8

Spicy Stewed Okra

Wrestling gators in the Bayou is tough work, so this spicy stewed okra fills the hunger gap. Big note: wrestling alligators is a risky bizness. Mind the teeth!

4 slices thick-cut bacon, diced

2 cloves garlic, minced

1 medium onion, diced

4 cups okra, cut in half lengthwise

1 tsp. Bayou Bite Cajun Rub (see page 44)

1 tsp. salt

2 cups drained canned chopped tomatoes

Pinch cayenne pepper

1. In a medium saucepan, fry the bacon, stirring frequently, until it is tender and the fat has rendered. Add the garlic, onion and okra; cook, stirring, for about 5 minutes. Stir in the Cajun Rub, salt and tomatoes with their juice. Cook over medium heat, stirring occasionally, until okra is tender and the mixture is thick, about 10 minutes. Season with cayenne pepper.
2. Serve hot over toast with smoked sausage.

Serves 6

Wok-Fried Spicy Sugar Snap Peas

Wokking should sometimes be called running, cuz you gotta move fast. High heat, quick cook time, and keep moving.

3 tbsp. peanut oil or vegetable oil

1 lb. sugar snap peas, trimmed

2 green onions, sliced

1 tsp. grated fresh ginger

1 tbsp. butter

1 tbsp. Sriracha chili sauce

Squeeze fresh lemon juice

Salt and pepper

1/4 cup coarsely ground peanuts

2 tbsp. torn cilantro leaves

1. Heat the wok over high heat until the pan is just smoking. Add the oil, peas, green onions and ginger; cook, stirring, until the peas are bright green. Stir in the butter and chili sauce. Add a squeeze of lemon juice and stir. Season to taste with salt and pepper. Remove from heat.
2. Toss with peanuts and cilantro leaves. Serve immediately.

Serves 4 to 6

Pan-Braised Swiss Chard

When I was a kid my Mom grew rows of Swiss chard in our little garden. She used to force-feed us this green guck. Man, I hated it. I can't believe it, but I now love Swiss chard.

2 bunches Swiss chard

2 tbsp. butter

1/4 cup chopped shallots

1 tsp. minced fresh ginger

1 tbsp. lime juice

1 tbsp. honey

1/4 cup cashew pieces

Salt and pepper

1. Trim the Swiss chard of any woody stalks. Roll the leaves and thinly slice crosswise. Wash the chard well in a sink of cold salted water. Drain well and spin to remove excess water.
2. In a large frying pan over high heat, melt the butter. Fry the shallots and ginger until tender, 1 to 2 minutes. Stir in the Swiss chard, cover and reduce heat to low. Cook for 10 to 15 minutes or until the chard is tender and most of the liquid is absorbed.
3. Stir in the lime juice, honey and cashews. Season to taste with salt and pepper. Serve immediately.

Serves 6

Slow-Roasted Garlic

Easy does it. Roasted garlic should appear golden brown and have a tender, sweet taste. Mmmm … Spread the soft garlic on buttered toast and sprinkle with sea salt. And the oil has a great flavour—use it for frying or in salad dressings.

1 cup peeled garlic cloves

1/2 cup vegetable oil

1. Preheat oven to 275°F.
2. Place the garlic and oil in a small baking dish, ensuring all the garlic is coated with oil. Bake for 30 minutes or until tender, stirring two or three times to ensure even browning. Let cool.
3. Pour garlic and oil into an airtight container. Roasted garlic and oil keep for 1 week, refrigerated.

Makes about 1/2 cup roasted garlic cloves and about 1 cup roasted garlic oil

Blackened Onions

Sweet onions and Cajun heat make these onions a perfect garnish for big juicy steaks.

2 medium sweet onions

1/4 cup melted butter

3 to 4 tbsp. Bayou Bite Cajun Rub (see page 44)

1. Line a baking sheet with foil. Slice the onions into 1/2-inch-thick rounds, keeping slices intact. Arrange slices on the baking sheet. Brush one side of the onions with about half of the melted butter. Dust liberally with about half of the Cajun seasoning, covering the entire surface of the onions. Turn onions over and repeat. Refrigerate to set the butter, about 10 minutes.
2. Meanwhile, preheat oven to 350°F.
3. In a well-ventilated kitchen, heat a large, heavy frying pan over high heat. (I like to use a cast-iron pan.) Fry the onions, a few slices at a time, until blackened, 2 to 3 minutes per side. Return onions as blackened to the cookie sheet.
4. Bake onions for 10 to 15 minutes or until tender.
5. Serve with blackened steaks and slices of smoked mozzarella cheese.

Serves 2 to 4

Banditos Baked Beans

This dish could also be considered a sausage and bean chili. It's a hearty winter warm-ya-upper.

4 ancho chilies, soaked and puréed

12 slices bacon, coarsely chopped

4 cloves garlic, minced

3 red or green jalapeño peppers, coarsely chopped

2 medium onions, coarsely chopped

1 poblano pepper, cut into 1/2-inch pieces

1 cubanelle pepper, cut into 1/2-inch pieces

2 stalks celery, cut into 1/2-inch pieces

2 cans (each 19 oz./540 mL) pinto beans, drained and rinsed

1 can (19 oz./540 mL) black-eyed peas, drained and rinsed

2 tbsp. Bone Dust BBQ Spice (see page 42)

2 tsp. ground cumin

1 cup salsa

1 cup Really Good Tomato Sauce (see page 73)

1/2 bottle beer

1 lb. smoked sausage (such as chorizo, Debraziner or kielbasa), cut into 1-inch chunks

1. Preheat oven to 350°F.
2. In a large oven-proof saucepan over medium-high heat, sauté the bacon until lightly crisp, 5 to 10 minutes. Add the garlic, jalapeño peppers, onions, poblano pepper, cubanelle pepper and celery. Sauté for 8 to 10 minutes or until tender.
3. Stir in the pinto beans, black-eyed peas, Bone Dust BBQ Spice, cumin, salsa, tomato sauce and beer. Bring to a boil. Cover and bake for 1 hour, stirring occasionally.
4. Stir in the sausage and cook, covered, for 1 hour, stirring occasionally.
5. Serve with ribs, fried chicken or burgers.

Serves 8 to 10

Old School Garlic Bread

When I first started cooking, I worked at the Old School Restaurant on Highway 2, between Paris and Brantford in Southern Ontario. We made a ton of garlic bread every day, along with gallons of French onion soup. To make these really cheesy, add a cup of shredded Swiss cheese.

1/2 lb. salted butter, just softened

1/4 cup grated Parmesan cheese

8 cloves garlic, minced

2 tbsp. chopped fresh chives

1 tsp. garlic salt

1 tsp. cracked black pepper

2 baguettes, cut in half lengthwise

1. Preheat oven to 350°F.
2. In a food processor, purée until smooth the butter, Parmesan cheese, garlic, chives, garlic salt and pepper. Spread liberally on each cut side of the baguette. Place top and bottom halves together and wrap tightly in foil. Bake for 40 minutes.
3. Carefully unwrap the garlic bread. Place bread buttered side up on a cookie sheet. Top with shredded cheese if you like. Broil for 2 to 3 minutes to lightly brown.
4. Slice and serve.

Serves 4 to 8 people

Desserts
and other
sinful treats

Desserts

Drinks

Warm Rice Pudding with Grilled Pineapple, Macadamia Nuts and Rum Syrup

Warm and fuzzy rice pudding: a dinner classic slightly modified.

1/2 cup maple syrup
1/4 cup dark rum
4 pineapple rings
1 cup Japanese short-grain rice
6 cups milk
2 cups heavy cream
1/2 cup sugar
1/2 vanilla bean
Pinch grated nutmeg
1 tsp. rum extract
1 cup table cream (18%)
1 cup toasted macadamia nuts

1. Preheat grill to medium-high.
2. Stir together the maple syrup and rum; set aside. Grill the pineapple, basting liberally with the rum syrup, for 3 to 4 minutes per side, until tender and lightly charred. Let cool slightly. Reserve the remaining syrup. Cut pineapple into 1-inch chunks and set aside.
3. In a medium saucepan, combine the rice, milk, heavy cream, sugar, vanilla bean, nutmeg and rum extract. Cover and bring to a slow boil over medium heat. Stir. Reduce heat to medium-low and simmer, covered, for 30 minutes, stirring occasionally. Uncover and simmer, stirring occasionally, for 15 minutes or until the rice is tender and the mixture has thickened. Remove from heat.
4. Discard the vanilla bean. Stir in the table cream. Cover surface with wax paper and let cool.
5. Spoon 1 cup of the rice pudding into each bowl and serve topped with the pineapple, macadamia nuts and additional rum syrup.

Serves 8

Bananas Flambé

While in St. Lucia, I made this dessert with a bottle of St. Lucia's finest Chairman's Reserve rum. I froze the rest of the rum for icy shots. Top this recipe off with Beer Caramel Sauce (see page 230).

3 tbsp. unsalted butter

4 small bananas, halved lengthwise

3 tbsp. brown sugar

2 tbsp. rum

1. In a heavy frying pan (not nonstick), melt the butter over medium-high heat. Sauté the bananas until tender and golden brown. Sprinkle with the sugar and cook, turning occasionally, for 2 to 3 minutes or until the bananas have caramelized.

2. Add the rum and light with a kitchen match. Be careful, as there can be a large flame. Flambé until the flames die out, about 30 seconds.

3. Serve over vanilla ice cream or ice cream bars.

Serves 4

Snickers Banana Bread Pudding with Beer Caramel Sauce

I wrote this recipe for Ontario's Beer Store magazine, *Chill*. Use more Snickers if you want 'cuz they're ooey gooey peanuty good. Caution: Beer Caramel Sauce may be addictive. It can also be used as a drizzling sauce with the one you love.

6 large eggs

2 cups heavy cream

1 cup milk

1/4 cup honey

1/2 tsp. ground cinnamon

1/2 tsp. vanilla extract

Pinch grated nutmeg

Pinch ground mace

2 cups ripe banana, halved lengthwise and cut into 1/2-inch slices (2 to 3 bananas)

2 Snickers bars, cut into 1/2-inch pieces

4 cups 1-inch cubes challah (about 8 slices)

Vanilla ice cream

1. Preheat oven to 350°F. Spray a 12 × 9-inch baking dish with nonstick cooking spray.
2. In a large bowl, whisk together the eggs, cream, milk, honey, cinnamon, vanilla, nutmeg and mace. Add the bananas, Snickers and bread; stir gently to allow the bread to absorb the liquid.
3. Spread the mixture evenly in the baking dish. Bake, uncovered, for 35 to 40 minutes or until the pudding is just set. Let cool for about 5 minutes before serving.
4. Spoon warm pudding into bowls. Add a scoop of vanilla ice cream and drizzle with Beer Caramel Sauce (see below).

Serves 6 to 8

Beer Caramel Sauce

2 bottles apple ale or honey lager

1 cup brown sugar

1 cup heavy cream

1/2 cup condensed milk

1. In a medium saucepan, boil the beer until reduced by half. Add the sugar; boil for 5 minutes, stirring, until the sugar has dissolved. Stir in the cream; boil for 5 more minutes. Let cool completely. Whisk in the condensed milk.
2. Serve over ice cream or bread pudding, or with fresh berries. Sauce keeps, refrigerated, for up to 5 days.

Makes 1 1/2 cups

Flourless Hot Liquid Magma Truffle Cake

My chef Mike McColl's wife, Mia, is a fantastic pastry chef. This is her kick-ass recipe. The truffle cake batter can be held refrigerated for 3 days and can be scooped cold into the ramekins.

12 large eggs

3/4 cup sugar

1/2 lb. dark chocolate, chopped

2 tbsp. unsalted butter

8 milk chocolate truffles

1. Preheat oven to 350°F. Grease eight 3-inch ramekins with butter or nonstick cooking spray and place on a baking sheet.
2. In a large bowl, whisk the eggs and sugar until the sugar is dissolved.
3. In the top of a double boiler over barely simmering water, melt the chocolate and butter, stirring to blend. Let chocolate cool for 5 minutes. Slowly pour the chocolate into the egg mixture, whisking until well blended. Divide the batter among the ramekins.
4. Push 1 truffle into the centre of each cake, making sure the truffle is covered with the batter.
5. Bake until the cake is firm but spongy and the chocolate centre is liquid, 10 to 12 minutes. (Some ovens might require a longer cooking time.)

Serves 8

Crème Brûlée Cheesecakes

My brother Jaimie drools over this recipe of my Mom's. It's the most awesome cheesecake recipe! Perfect for dipping and licking.

5 large eggs

4 pkg. (each 8 oz./250 g) cream cheese

2 cups sour cream

1/2 cup unsalted butter

1 1/4 cups sugar

Seeds from 1/2 vanilla bean OR 1 1/4 tsp. vanilla extract

1 tsp. fresh lemon juice

2 tbsp. cornstarch

1/2 cup brown sugar

1 pint fresh raspberries

1 pint fresh blackberries

Icing sugar

Special equipment: kitchen blowtorch

1. Let the eggs, cream cheese, sour cream, butter and eggs stand at room temperature for about 1 hour.
2. Preheat oven to 375°F. Butter eight 4-inch ramekins.
3. In a large bowl, blend the cream cheese, sour cream, butter and sugar until smooth. Stir together the vanilla seeds and lemon juice until the vanilla seeds no longer clump. Add the vanilla mixture and cornstarch to the cream cheese mixture. Using an electric mixer, beat on medium-high speed until well blended. Beat in the eggs, one at a time, and beat until the mixture is very smooth.
4. Pour the batter into the ramekins, smoothing the surface. Put the ramekins in a baking dish or roasting pan and add hot water to come halfway up the sides of the ramekins. Bake for 20 to 30 minutes or until the tops are golden brown and the insides are still a little runny.
5. Turn off oven and let cakes cool with oven door open for 20 minutes. Remove from water bath and let stand at room temperature for 30 minutes. (Cheesecakes may be chilled at this point, if that's the way you prefer to eat them.)
6. Sprinkle the top of each cheesecake with an even layer of the brown sugar. Using a kitchen blowtorch, carefully caramelize the sugar until it is melted and golden brown, but not burnt. Top each with an assortment of fresh berries and a dusting of icing sugar.

Serves 8

Peach and Bourbon Cobbler

This recipe is dedicated to my brother and sister-in-law, Matt and Sig, in appreciation for all of the wild peach chases that I have sent you on. Cheers!

The "Cob"

4 cups sliced peeled fresh peaches (about 12 peaches)

1/2 cup fresh blueberries

1/4 cup bourbon

1 tsp. vanilla extract

3/4 cup sugar

3 tbsp. tapioca starch

Pinch salt

The "Bler"

1/4 cup butter, softened

1/2 cup sugar

1 large egg

1 1/2 cups all-purpose flour

2 tsp. baking powder

Pinch salt

1/2 cup table cream (18%)

1. To make the "Cob," in a large bowl, stir together the peaches, blueberries, bourbon and vanilla. Let sit for 1 hour.
2. Add the sugar, tapioca starch and salt. Stir well and set aside.
3. Preheat oven to 425°F. Butter a 9 × 6-inch baking dish.
4. To make the "Bler," in a stand mixer, cream the butter. Add the sugar and beat until smooth. Add the egg and beat until smooth. Sift together the flour, baking powder and salt. Add flour mixture and cream alternately to the butter mixture in three batches, beating until smooth.
5. Evenly spread the "Cob" in the baking dish. Pour the "Bler" over the "Cob." Bake for 30 to 40 minutes, until topping is golden brown and set. Let cool for 10 minutes before serving.
6. Serve spooned over vanilla ice cream.

Serves 6 to 8

Joe Louis Ice Cream Burger

Every once in a while I make these burgers for my nieces and nephews—it's great fun for kids, and adults too. If you're a Canadian you'll know about the Joe Louis snack cake. If you're from the U.S.A., use Moon Pies or even a Twinkie.

1/2 cup fresh raspberries
1/2 cup fresh blueberries
1 tbsp. sugar
1 tbsp. Grand Marnier
4 Joe Louis snack cakes
4 tsp. raspberry jam
1 Snickers bar, cut into cubes
1/4 cup milk chocolate chips
2 tbsp. condensed milk
4 scoops vanilla ice cream
1 cup whipped cream or whipped topping
Beer Caramel Sauce (see page 230)

1. In a bowl, stir together the raspberries, blueberries, sugar and Grand Marnier; set aside.
2. Cut the Joe Louis cakes in half. Spread 1 tsp. of the jam on the bottom half of each cake.
3. In a microwave-safe dish, combine the Snickers pieces, chocolate chips and condensed milk. Microwave, uncovered, on Medium for 30 seconds; stir. Microwave for 30 seconds more; stir again. Spread Snickers mixture onto the other half of each Joe Louis. Place a scoop of ice cream on each jam-topped cake half. Top ice cream with Snickers-smeared cake half.
4. Garnish with whipped cream and the berries, drizzle with Beer Caramel Sauce, and serve immediately.

Serves 4

Vacation Shake

A delicious banana daiquiri shake made with rum, rum and rum with bananas, ice cream and (oh yeah) rum. Mmmmmm. For any time of any day!

1 ripe banana, sliced
2 scoops vanilla ice cream
1/4 cup coconut milk
1 oz. spiced rum
1 oz. dark rum
1/2 oz. banana rum or liqueur
Coffee liqueur, for drizzling

Reserve 1 banana slice for garnish. In a blender, blend the banana, ice cream, coconut milk, spiced rum, dark rum and banana rum until smooth. Pour into a fancy shmancy frozen glass. Drizzle with coffee liqueur. Garnish with the banana slice, cocktail umbrella and a straw for sucking. Drink and repeat! Happy holidays!

Makes 1

Gold Miner's Yukon Martini

Even the roughest and toughest gold miner from da Great White North would like this hoity-toity martini.

2 oz. vodka, chilled
1 oz. Yukon Jack
1/2 oz. Goldschlager (cinnamon schnapps)
Golden raspberries, for garnish

Put 3 or 4 ice cubes in a martini shaker. Pour in vodka, Yukon Jack and Goldschlager. Shake well. Strain into a chilled martini glass. Garnish with golden raspberries and drink.

Serves 1

Tequila Shots with Watermelon Ice Cubes (a.k.a. Brain-Freeze Shooters)

One of my favourite cocktails is a chilled shot of naked tequila, and not just any tequila. I am a big fan of artisanal small-batch tequilas made from 100% blue agave. Whether it be reposado (a lightly oak-barrel-aged tequila) or an añejo (aged at least one year), I like my tequila chilled in the freezer so that it is almost syruplike. I find chilling enhances the flavours of the tequila. This combo is a refreshing summer treat and less fuss than the almighty margarita.

1 bottle reposado tequila

1 small seedless watermelon

1. Place the tequila bottle and two shot glasses in the freezer for at least 4 hours. (Don't worry, the tequila will not be frozen solid, it will just be *really* cold.)
2. Meanwhile, line a cookie sheet with plastic wrap. Peel the watermelon. Cut into 1 1/2-inch cubes. Arrange watermelon cubes on the cookie sheet and freeze for 30 minutes or until the watermelon is just beginning to crystallize but is not frozen.
3. Pour tequila into frozen shot glasses. Shoot tequila. Suck, chew and swallow watermelon cubes. Rub forehead due to "brain pain." Repeat.

Serves 2 plus

Aphrodite's Goddess of Love Drops

Try these love poppers to enhance your lovemaking, if ya know what I mean. Works best during cold winter nights with the one you love. Hubba, hubba.

1 bunch seedless grapes, rinsed

1/2 cup ouzo

1. Remove grapes from stems and place in a bowl. Add ouzo and toss. Pour into a shallow dish and refrigerate for 2 to 4 hours.
2. Line a baking sheet with plastic wrap. Using a slotted spoon, remove the grapes from the ouzo and place evenly on the baking sheet. Have a shot or two of the ouzo. Freeze the grapes until firm, 2 to 3 hours.
3. Enjoy the grapes as refreshing grape poppers.

Serves 2

Tip: This works well with other liqueurs. Try amaretto, Grand Marnier, rum or limoncello.

Index